TEACHER'S GUIDE

Focus: Nonfiction

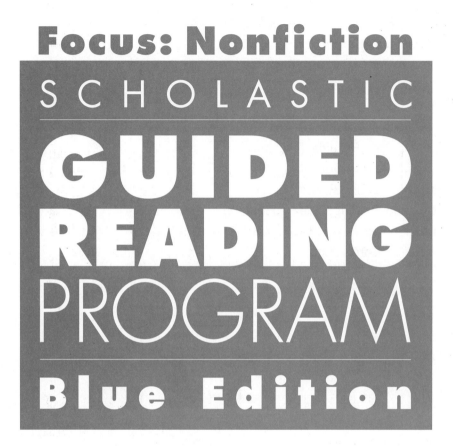

SCHOLASTIC

GUIDED READING PROGRAM

Blue Edition

by Gay Su Pinnell
The Ohio State University

Copyright © 2002 Scholastic Inc.   All rights reserved.   Published by Scholastic Inc.   Printed in the U.S.A.
ISBN 0-439-44657-0
SCHOLASTIC, *SCHOLASTIC READING COUNTS!* and associated logos and designs
are trademarks and/or registered trademarks of Scholastic Inc.
LEXILE is a trademark of MetaMetrics, Inc.
14 15 16 17 18 19 20 21 22 23 24   40   11 10 09 08 07

TABLE OF CONTENTS

Guided Reading

Characteristics of Text

Additional Resources

USING YOUR
GUIDED READING PROGRAM

The *Scholastic Guided Reading Program* is a varied collection of books that are categorized by the kind and level of challenge they offer students as they are learning to read. The Guided Reading Program consists of 260 books organized into 26 levels of difficulty—Levels A–Z. Many different characteristics of the texts are considered in determining the level of challenge and support a particular book or shorter story presents.

Advantages of a Leveled Book Collection
A leveled book set has many advantages, including the following:

- **It provides experience with a wide variety of texts within a level.**
- **It makes it easier to select books for groups of children.**
- **It lends itself to flexible grouping.**
- **It provides a way to assess children's progress.**
- **It provides a basic book collection that can be expanded over time.**

Multiple Copies of Books

Six copies of each book are provided so that students in small groups will have access to their own copies. Having a collection of books on various levels, with multiple copies of each book, allows you to consider individual strengths when grouping and selecting books. To help you identify a book's level quickly, you may place a Guided Reading Program sticker for the level on each book cover.

Flexibility of Use

With a gradient of text, grouping can be more flexible. Students might read only some of the books in a level, and not necessarily in the same sequence. In addition, children may change groups based on individual needs. The **Characteristics of Text** and **Behaviors to Notice and Support**, on pages 32–57, will assist you in placing children in the appropriate levels.

If you note that some students need extra support for a particular text or that the selection is too difficult for most of the group, you can abandon guided reading and instead use shared reading to experience the book. Then you can select an easier book the next day. As students progress, have them reread books on a lower level for enjoyment. Students will become more confident readers as they reread a book for meaning with no need for problem solving.

Adding to the Guided Reading Program

The Guided Reading Program has been designed with adaptability in mind, so you may add copies of children's and your own favorite books to the library. You may place a Guided Reading Program sticker for the suggested level on each book you add.

Variety Within Levels in the Collection

When working with groups in classroom reading, a broad base of text is needed. The Guided Reading Program provides this broad base. Readers who experience only one kind of book may develop a narrow range of strategies for processing text. With a leveled set, difficulty is controlled because all text characteristics have been factored in. Yet the level of text is not artificially controlled because the variety of text characteristics occurs within natural story language.

The early levels of the Guided Reading Program introduce students to reading print. While reading at these beginning levels, students apply phonics skills, develop a core of high-frequency words, work with print in a variety of layouts, and engage with a variety of high-interest texts.

Books at later levels (Levels J and beyond) include a wider range of text. Within each level, literary texts are included. Essentially, there are three kinds of books at these levels, although there is variety within each category.

- **First, there are longer stories and chapter books—mostly narratives that present increasingly complex plots and memorable characters. These longer selections provide an opportunity for readers to sustain reading over time, remembering details, and getting to know characters as they develop.**
- **Second, there are informational books which are generally shorter. These present complex ideas and some technical language. They challenge students to acquire and discuss ideas and information and to go beyond the text to research topics of interest to them.**
- **Third, there are picture books at a more sophisticated level than before. These picture books provide an opportunity to expand vocabulary, to interpret stories, and to recognize how illustrations contribute to the story. Like the short story, picture books provide the advanced reader complex reading material that does not take several days to complete.**

FACTORS CONSIDERED IN
LEVELING BOOKS

In placing a book, short story, or article along a gradient of text, multiple characteristics of text are considered. Here is a sample list.

Book and Print Features
Refers to the physical aspects of the text—what readers cope with in terms of length, size, print layout, and font size. It also refers to the interpretation of illustrations and the relationships between information in graphics and the body of the text.

- How many words are in the book?
- How many lines of text are on each page?
- How many pages are in the book?
- What size is the print?
- How much space is there between words and lines?
- How easy is it to find information?
- What is the relationship between print and illustrations?
- Are there graphics (photos, diagrams, maps) that provide essential information and how easy are the graphics to interpret?
- What are the features of print layout? (For example, do sentences begin on the left or do they "wrap around" so that end punctuation must be relied upon?)
- Is print placed in standard, predictable places on the pages or is it used in creative ways that require the reader's flexibility?
- Do size and shape of book, binding, and layout play a role in text interpretation?

Genre
Means the "type" or "kind" and refers to a classification system formed to provide a way of talking about what texts are like (fiction—including realistic fiction, fantasy, traditional literature; and nonfiction—including biography, autobiography, and informational texts).

- What is the "genre" or "kind" of book?
- What special demands does this genre make on readers?
- Is this an easy or more difficult example of the genre?

Content
Refers to the subject matter that readers are required to understand as they read both fiction and nonfiction texts.

- What background information is essential for understanding this text?
- What new information will readers need to grasp to read the text?
- How accessible is the content to the readers?

Themes and Ideas
Refers to the "big picture," the universality of the problem in the text and its relevance to peoples' lives.

- What is the theme of the text?
- Are there multiple themes that the reader must understand and be able to talk about?
- How accessible are the "big ideas" to the reader?

Language and Literary Features

Refers to the writer's style and use of literary devices. Literary features are those elements typically used in literature to capture imagination, stir emotions, create empathy or suspense, give readers a sense that characters and story are real, and make readers care about the outcome of the plot. Nonfiction books may incorporate some literary features.

- From what perspective is the story or informational text written?
- To what degree does the writer use literary language, such as metaphor?
- To what degree does the writer use sophisticated literary devices, such as flashbacks or stories within stories?
- How engaging and authentic is the dialogue?
- Is dialogue assigned (using *he said*) or unassigned with longer stretches of interchange that the reader must follow and attribute to one character or another?
- How are characters revealed through what they say or think and what others say or think about them?
- How easy is it to understand the characters and their motivations and development?
- Is character development essential to the story?
- How essential to the story are understandings about setting and plot?

Vocabulary and Words

Refers to the words and their accessibility to readers. Vocabulary generally refers to the meaning of words that readers may decode but not understand. Word solving refers to both decoding and to understanding meaning.

- What is the frequency of multisyllabic words in the text?
- How complex are word meanings? (For example, are readers required to understand multiple meanings or subtle shades of meaning of words?)
- What prior knowledge is needed to understand the vocabulary of the text?
- How many content or technical words are included in the text?

Sentence Complexity

Refers to the syntactic patterns readers will encounter in the text; sentences may be simple (short, with one subject and predicate) or complex (longer, with embedded clauses).

- What is the average length of sentences in the text?
- To what degree do sentences contain embedded clauses?
- What is the sentence style of the writer?
- Are there complex sentences joined by *and*, *but*, or other conjunctions?
- Are paragraphs organized so that readers can recognize lead sentences and main ideas?

Punctuation

Refers to the graphic symbols that signal the way text should be read to reflect the author's meaning.

- What punctuation symbols are used in the text?
- What do readers need to notice about punctuation in order to fully understand the text?
- What punctuation is essential for readers to notice to read with fluency and phrasing?

Using Leveled Books With Readers

The success of guided reading depends on many factors other than text characteristics. These, of course, have to do with the young readers using the texts as well as teacher-student interactions and include:

- **The reader's prior knowledge of the topic, including vocabulary and concepts.**
- **The reader's prior experience with texts that have similar features.**
- **The way the teacher introduces the text.**
- **The supportive interactions between the teacher and children before, during, and after reading.**
- **The level of interest teachers help students build.**

Level-by-Level Descriptions

Characteristics of text for each level in the Guided Reading Program are listed on pages 32–57. These descriptions are general: not every book included in a level will have every characteristic noted. Also listed are some important behaviors to notice and support at each level. As you use these books with children, you will notice how they support and challenge students.

Other Resources

You may want to refer to the following resources for descriptions of guided reading as well as additional books for each level:

- Fountas, Irene, and Pinnell, G.S. 1996. *Guided Reading: Good First Teaching for All Children*. Portsmouth, NH: Heinemann.
- Fountas, Irene, and Pinnell, G.S. 1999. *Matching Books to Readers: A Leveled Book List for Guided Reading, K–3*. Portsmouth, NH: Heinemann.
- Fountas, Irene, and Pinnell, G.S. 1999. *Voices on Word Matters.* Portsmouth, NH: Heinemann.
- Pinnell, Gay Su and Fountas, I.C. 1998. *Word Matters: Teaching Phonics and Spelling in the Reading/Writing Classroom*. Portsmouth, NH: Heinemann.

WHAT IS
GUIDED READING?

Guided reading is an instructional approach that involves a teacher working with a small group of students who demonstrate similar reading behaviors and can all read similar levels of texts. The text is easy enough for students to read with your skillful support. The text offers challenges and opportunities for problem solving, but is easy enough for students to read with some fluency. You choose selections that help students expand their strategies.

What is the purpose of guided reading?

You select books that students can read with about 90 percent accuracy. Students can understand and enjoy the story because it's accessible to them through their own strategies, supported by your introduction. They focus on meaning but use problem-solving strategies to figure out words they don't know, deal with difficult sentence structure, and understand concepts or ideas they have never before encountered in print.

Why is guided reading important?

Guided reading gives students the chance to apply the strategies they already know to new text. You provide support, but the ultimate goal is independent reading.

When are children ready for guided reading?

Developing readers have already gained important understandings about how print works. These students know how to monitor their own reading. They have the ability to check on themselves or search for possibilities and alternatives if they encounter a problem when reading. For these readers, the guided reading experience is a powerful way to support the development of reading strategies.

The ultimate goal of guided reading is reading a variety of texts with ease and deep understanding. Silent reading means rapid processing of texts with most attention on meaning, which is achieved as readers move past beginning levels (H, I, J). At all levels, students read orally with fluency and phrasing.

Matching Books to Readers

The teacher selects a text for a small group of students who are similar in their reading behaviors at a particular point in time. In general, the text is about right for students in the group. It is not too easy, yet not too hard, and offers a variety of challenges to help readers become flexible problem solvers. You should choose Guided Reading Program books for students that:

- match their knowledge base.
- help them take the next step in learning to read.
- are interesting to them.
- offer just enough challenge to support problem solving while still supporting fluency and meaning.

Supporting Students' Reading

In working with students in guided reading, you constantly balance the difficulty of the text with support for students reading the text. You introduce the story to the group, support individuals through brief interactions while they read, and guide them to talk together afterwards about the words and ideas in the text. In this way, you refine text selection and help individual readers move forward in developing a reading process.

Good readers employ a wide range of word-solving strategies, including analysis of sound-letter relationships and word parts. They must figure out words that are embedded in different kinds of texts. Reading a variety of books enables them to go beyond reading individual words to interpreting language and its subtle meanings.

For more specific teaching suggestions, see individual cards for each book title.

Procedure for Guided Reading

- The teacher works with a small group of students with similar needs.
- The teacher provides introductions to the text that support children's later attempts at problem solving.
- Each student reads the whole text or a unified part of the text.
- Readers figure out new words while reading for meaning.
- The teacher prompts, encourages, and confirms students' attempts at problem solving.
- The teacher and student engage in meaningful conversations about what they are reading.
- The teacher and student revisit the text to demonstrate and use a range of comprehension strategies.

ORGANIZING YOUR CLASSROOM FOR GUIDED READING

adapted from *Guided Reading: Making It Work* (Schulman and Payne, 2000)

Good management begins with a thoughtful room arrangement and careful selection of materials; the way you organize furniture and supplies will support the learning that takes place within your classroom. For guided reading to be effective, the rest of the class must be engaged in other literacy activities that do not require direct teacher involvement. For most classes, this means literacy centers that accommodate small groups of students. So, a strategically-arranged classroom for guided reading would have a class library, inviting spots for individual work, spaces for whole-class gatherings and small-group meetings, and several literacy centers.

Arranging the room and organizing materials for effective reading and writing workshops takes thought and planning. So before the school year even begins, consider the activities you're planning for your class and the physical layout of your room. With a little ingenuity, you can provide an environment that will support learning all year long.

Scheduling for Guided Reading

To determine the time you'll need for guided reading, consider the number of students in your class and the range of reading abilities they possess. Then create your initial groupings; the ideal group size is four to six, though guided reading groups might range from three to eight. Place below-grade or struggling readers in smaller groups. Keep in mind that sessions are short—often 10–15 minutes for emergent readers, and 15–30 minutes for more advanced readers. You will want to meet with at-risk groups every day; five meetings over a two-week period for more advanced groups is typical. You'll also want to allow yourself some time for assessment—taking a running record, jotting anecdotal notes, or conducting oral interviews, for example. Finally, allow a few minutes between groups to check in with the rest of the class.

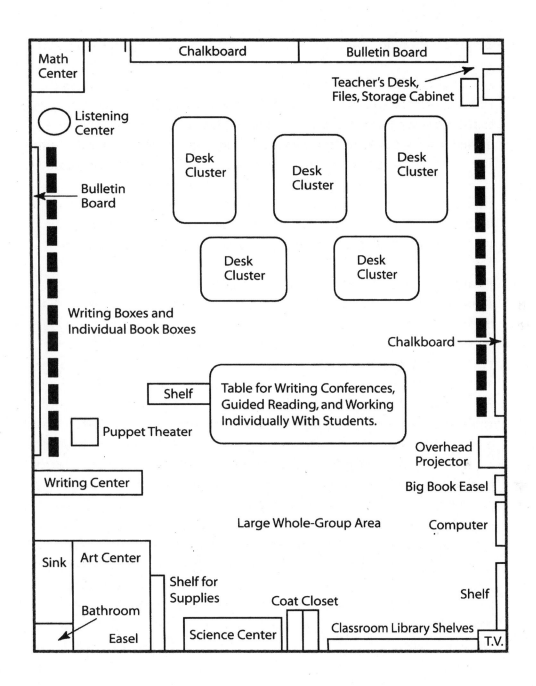

Math Center

Chalkboard

Bulletin Board

Teacher's Desk, Files, Storage Cabinet

Listening Center

Desk Cluster

Desk Cluster

Desk Cluster

Bulletin Board

Desk Cluster

Desk Cluster

Writing Boxes and Individual Book Boxes

Chalkboard

Shelf

Table for Writing Conferences, Guided Reading, and Working Individually With Students.

Puppet Theater

Overhead Projector

Big Book Easel

Writing Center

Large Whole-Group Area

Computer

Sink

Art Center

Shelf for Supplies

Coat Closet

Shelf

Bathroom

Classroom Library Shelves

Easel

Science Center

T.V.

SETTING UP
LITERACY CENTERS

adapted from *Guided Reading: Making It Work* (Schulman and Payne, 2000)

As a way of managing the time to meet with small groups of students, teachers often use literacy centers. At literacy centers, students continue to participate in purposeful and authentic literacy activities. These centers provide many opportunities to practice the skills real readers and writers use. They take the place of traditional worksheets and are not meant to be graded.

Literacy centers can be designed to address a wide range of skills levels, learning styles, and interests. Students work in heterogeneous groups that change often. The number of students at each center depends upon the type of center and the space for it. For example, in one first-grade classroom, the listening center has stations for four students, the computer center accommodates one student per computer, and the library center holds up to three students.

When arranging your centers, consider the number of students you want to accommodate at once, the space you have available, and the topics that you want to cover. Also think about transitions between centers—will students work at the same center during the whole guided reading period? If so, do they know what to do if they finish early? If not, do they know how to move to another center or activity without disturbing you or other class members? Establishing clear expectations and routines will help centers run smoothly, so you can focus on guided reading groups.

When first setting up students' use of literacy centers, take time each day to discuss with students what happened at centers that day. Some questions to consider are, "What went well? What might we change to make it work better?" This helps students think about ways to problem-solve when they meet difficulties working independently.

Things to Consider When Setting Up Literacy Centers

- Establish a manageable number of centers that can be changed easily and routinely.
- Plan time to introduce and demonstrate how each center operates. Some teachers do this during scheduled shared reading/writing time.
- Consider the physical arrangement of the centers to permit movement and a balance of quiet and noisy areas.
- Design centers to meet the range of all learners, addressing a variety of interests and learning styles.
- Have supplies accessible and labeled for independent student use.
- Create signs or charts that communicate functional information and directions, such as "How to Use the Audiocassette Player."
- Develop a plan for the rotation of students through centers and a way to keep track of centers.
- Provide an opportunity for students to select centers.
- Develop a signal or a problem-solving technique for students to use while they are at centers and you are working with other students.
- Periodically review what's working and not working at centers.

Managing and Organizing Literacy Centers

There are a variety of ways to organize and manage centers. Some teachers have students select literacy centers, while others choose the centers for the students to ensure they regularly rotate through them. No matter which approach you take, it is important to have a record-keeping system in place to monitor student participation in various centers.

GROUPING STUDENTS

Your job is to take each student from his or her present level to a more advanced one. Therefore, there must be assessment of individual students. With class sizes ranging from 20 to 35, grouping for instruction makes sense. As teachers, we want to make learning manageable, while avoiding any negative aspects of grouping.

Fundamentals of Grouping

Assessment of Students' Knowledge Base

Students' knowledge base is the key element in selecting texts and planning instruction for groups so that they can read with 90 percent accuracy and use the skills that assure understanding. Other aspects to consider when selecting the best level for a group include:

- **how well developing readers can control a strategy, such as analyzing a new word.**
- **the kinds of language students find understandable and which they find challenging.**
- **what concepts they know or what concepts they don't understand.**
- **the kinds of texts and genres they have experienced. For example, if they have handled only narrative texts, then informational texts may be difficult.**

See pages 32–57 for help in assessing which level is best for a group.

Dynamic Grouping

Because students' individual needs change so often, ongoing observation of behavior and assessment of their knowledge and experience are essential to the guided reading process. Students progress at different rates, so regrouping is also ongoing. By grouping in different ways for different purposes, you can avoid labeling students with group names that are symbols of a static achievement level.

As you informally assess students' reading on a daily basis, you may wish to use the descriptions of **Behaviors to Notice and Support** on pages 32–57 for the level of book you are using. A quick, informal observation of students' reading will help you determine if the book was at the appropriate level.

- **Was this book too hard for this student? If the child can't read it independently with 85–95 percent accuracy and isn't using strategies as he or she reads, then the book is too hard.**
- **If the student reads with such fluency that there is no need for problem-solving behaviors, then the student should be reading a higher-level text for guided reading. Of course, the lower-level text will be useful for fluency practice.**

RUNNING GUIDED READING GROUPS

Step 1   **Select a Book**

With students' needs in mind, select a book for a group of two to six. Use the **Characteristics of Text** to determine general level appropriateness and the description of **Behaviors to Notice and Support** to determine if students' reading ability matches that level. (See pages 32–57)

Depending on available time, each group of readers at levels A–J might read two to five new books a week. As texts become longer, readers will read fewer books but must sustain attention and memory over several days or a week of reading. For readers in grades 3–6, the goal of independent and guided reading instruction is to enable students to read one chapter book a week or several shorter selections. No two groups will read exactly the same sequence of books, and groups will change as the assessment system helps track progress.

Step 2   **Introduce the Book**

Introducing the story is probably the most important and most difficult part of guided reading, and it is your opportunity to provide most of the support to the reader. A brief introduction helps a group to read successfully with minimal teacher support. You may tailor the introduction based on the group and the particular text. Depending on the level of difficulty and students' reading abilities, the introduction includes any combination of these elements:

- **a short conversation about the main idea of the text.**
- **a briefing on the author's purpose for writing and some important features of the plot.**
- **a description of the main characters in the story.**
- **a presentation of any unusual or unique language, such as a repetitive refrain.**
- **a discussion of concepts needed for understanding of text by activating prior knowledge.**
- **drawing attention to any aspects of print that you consider important.**
- **getting students to predict what they think will happen.**
- **instructions on how much to read and what to do when finished.**

Without actually reading the text to students, frame it in a meaningful way. Using oral language in a way that familiarizes students with some words they will meet in print helps prepare them to read. It isn't necessary to introduce every page, preteach words, or give a purpose for reading. The idea is to help students to be able to move through the text on their own. Any brief intervention should not interfere with the momentum of independent reading.

Step 3 Read the Book

Once the book has been introduced, students are ready to read. Unlike round-robin reading, in which each student reads a page or sentence, each student using guided reading reads the entire text.

- **Each student reads independently and problem-solves on his or her own.**
- **Reading may be oral or silent, depending on level and skill.**

As students read, you are nearby to observe them, providing support when necessary. As they read, note reading behaviors and offer praise when students use a strategy successfully. More advanced students will be reading silently. You can sample their oral reading by asking them to lift their voices to an audible level for a page or two. All students continue reading silently at their own rates as you sample oral reading from several of them.

If students have been placed in the appropriate level, they will problem-solve independently. However, if the whole group seems stuck, you may want to stop the group to assist in problem solving. You might also make teaching points, such as pointing out inflectional endings or consonant digraphs. Detours should be brief, not interrupting the momentum of students' reading.

Try to choose one student in the group daily to observe and interact with, helping him or her develop reading strategies, and encouraging the independent use of those strategies.

Step 4 ## Respond to the Book and Learn about Reading

After students read, first invite them to discuss the meaning of the text. Then select one or two teaching points to bring to their attention. What you select to teach depends on students' needs. You might focus on the meaning of a portion of text, on character interpretation, on humor, or on some aspect of word solving, such as multisyllabic words. For example, you might:

- promote fluency and phrasing by asking students to read aloud a favorite part of the story or a portion of dialogue as that character might speak it.
- help students focus on key ideas and language by having them find a turning point in the story, a humorous part, or a description of a character's feelings.
- help students figure out new, longer words by having them focus on word parts or known words.
- engage students in actively exploring how words work—building words, changing words, and noticing their features.

By following up the reading of a text in this way, you are helping students develop strategies that they can apply to the reading of other books. You are helping them learn the "how to" of reading and to move forward toward the goal of developing a reading process.

Step 5 ## Assess Behavior

The day after a new text is read, record the ability level of one child and note any progress. The **Behaviors to Notice and Support** can help you assess.

USING THE **GUIDED READING** TEACHING CARDS

The author, genre, level, and word count (for Levels A–K) are provided.

All texts have features that make it easier for the reader to make meaning. Those features are highlighted to assist you as you guide students through the book.

A summary is included to familiarize yourself with the book or give you a brief reminder of its content.

SCHOLASTIC
GUIDED READING PROGRAM

Dive!
My Adventures in the Deep Frontier

by Sylvia A. Earle
genre: science non-fiction
Level W

Summary In this photo essay, marine biologist and ocean explorer Sylvia Earle combines personal adventure and scientific facts to recount her many experiences diving in the world's oceans. Color photographs show the author eye to eye with everything from a humpback whale to a wild dolphin and a squid. She also describes walking on the ocean floor in a special diving suit, exploring deep coral reefs in a special submersible machine, and living for two weeks in an underwater "space station."

Background Information

Jacques Cousteau, a French oceanographer, helped to develop the aqualung in 1943. This device made it possible for divers to swim underwater for extended periods of time without coming up for air. In addition to the aqualung, he developed the first underwater diving station and an underwater observation vehicle called the diving saucer. Beginning in 1951, Cousteau explored the oceans on his ship *Calypso*, writing a number of books on sea life and producing several motion pictures as well.

For more information on underwater exploration, see the web site of the National Aquarium in Baltimore at www.aqua.org.

Supportive Text Features

Dive! contains a glossary of terms that are related to oceanography, such as *bathyscaphe* and *snorkel*. In addition, a number of full-color photographs fully illustrate the different kinds of diving gear the author describes, as well as the startling variety of undersea life found around the world.

Praise students for specific use of "Behaviors to Notice and Support" on page 54 of the *Guided Reading Teacher's Guide*.

Challenging Text Features

A number of words that might otherwise give students difficulty can be defined if they use the photographs in the book as well as context clues. For example, in the phrase *simply hover, mid-water, like a jellyfish* on page 14, the word *hover* can be easily defined if students use the visual clue in the photograph on page 6.

Some students may have prior knowledge gaps that will impede comprehension. The background information is included to be shared with students prior to reading. Use the information to determine students' level of background knowledge. Clarify or add to existing knowledge. In addition, a web site is provided for further research and resources.

Even simple books may contain text features that may hinder a student's comprehension. These are noted so that you can be on the "lookout" for them as students read, and assist students in dealing with challenging features.

Lessons for one to two comprehension strategies are provided. In each lesson, the skill is defined and sample questions are included for you to teach the skill and assess students' mastery.

TEACHING OPTIONS

Comprehension Strategies
Recognizing Main Idea/Details
The main idea is the most important point an author makes in a paragraph, passage, or selection. If the main idea is stated directly in the text, it is explicit. If it is not directly stated, it is implicit, and readers must put the main idea into their own words. Finding the main idea in each chapter of the book can help readers summarize the material.

- In the first chapter, Sylvia Earle talks about her fascination with the sea when she was growing up. I don't think the main idea is stated directly in the text though. What is the main idea of this first chapter?
- Sylvia Earle feels that whales are treasures that, once gone, can never be replaced. What details in Chapter 2 support this idea?
- Sylvia Earle talks about many different topics in this book—undersea plants and fish, and the importance of protecting the oceans. How would you sum it all up into one main idea?

Understanding Genre:
Science Nonfiction
Science nonfiction informs readers about actual places, people, and events that are related to a science topic. Graphic devices such as photographs, diagrams, charts, sidebars, and maps help the author explain the material.

- How do the map and chart on pages 12 and 14 help you to understand the information Sylvia Earle presents in this book?
- Hundreds of years went by before people made any advances on the inventions of the Greek sponge divers. What other conclusions can you draw from the time line on page 60?

Phonics and Word-Solving Strategy
Identifying Open and Closed Syllables
Remind students that words are made up of syllables and that each syllable has one vowel sound. An open syllable ends with a vowel and usually has a long vowel sound. A closed syllable ends with a consonant, and the vowel sound is usually short.

- Write the following words on the chalkboard. Divide each word by syllables using slash marks. (fish/es, mo/tion/less) **fishes, algae, seaweed, propulsion, bubbles, diving, scuba, krill, motionless**
- Ask students to read the words aloud and identify the number of syllables in each word.
- Have students identify which syllables in each word are closed, and which are open.

Oral Language/Vocabulary
- Ask students to note which of the sea life discussed in the book interested them the most, and then discuss with them which part of the ocean they might like to explore.
- Discuss with students other books they have read in which the sea plays a prominent role. Have them compare the experiences with those described in *Dive!*

Extending Meaning Through Reading and Writing
- Have students write about a fish or marine mammal described in the book. Tell students that their paragraph should include the animal's physical features, behavior, or habitat. **(Expository)**
- Have students reread their favorite chapter in the book. Then invite students to write their own interview with Earle, using the material in the text to fashion both questions and answers. **(Expository)**

Fluency Practice
Model fluent reading of a passage from the book, stressing appropriate pauses that would occur at the ends of sentences and before commas. Then have everyone read the passage together.

Much can be done to build students' listening and speaking vocabularies. This section engages students in conversations about the book to check their comprehension, use newly-learned words, and extend understanding.

Reading and writing are reciprocal processes. Writing prompts for narrative, expository, descriptive, and persuasive writing are provided. Some help to further assess comprehension of text. Others offer writing process prompts for fuller, richer writing experiences.

Lessons for one to two phonics and word-solving strategies are also provided. These lessons will help students decode unfamiliar words and use their knowledge of common spelling patterns as they read.

This section offers fluency-building ctivities. Students need opportunities to read and reread books to develop their automaticity with word recognition. In addition, they need opportunities to hear fluent reading models and discuss the importance of fluency, and guided practice sessions to develop fluency.

ASSESSMENT
OBSERVATION

Overview

We define assessment as the collection of information about a student's learning, and evaluation as the judgment about the student's strengths and specific needs based on this information. Assessment should be continuous—based on observation and informal measures of reading performance. Evaluation should provide a guide for teaching decisions that will help the student's learning.

To assess and evaluate a student's literacy development, information needs to be collected to demonstrate the following:

- **how a student uses and responds to oral language in various settings.**
- **what a student knows about reading and writing.**
- **how a student uses reading and writing in various settings.**
- **how a student values reading and writing.**

The Guided Reading Program is structured to give information on different kinds of literacy skills for children with varied learning needs. The program supports literacy development in reading, writing, listening, and speaking. These literacy activities provide a wealth of assessment information.

Purposes of Assessment

As a student progresses from a beginning reader and writer to a fluent reader and writer, assessment may have several purposes:

- **to establish what a student initially knows about literacy.**
- **to identify a student's instructional reading level.**
- **to monitor a student's pattern of strengths.**

Assessment needs to take place at the beginning of the school year to know what foundational skills students have and to identify potential skill needs. All school-age children know something about oral and written language and are ready to learn more. Some may have knowledge about environmental print but little experience with books or with writing. Others may be confident with books and with some writing.

Observation

One of the best ways to assess an individual student's learning is through observation. For a well-rounded view of the student, try to observe him or her throughout the day in a variety of settings, such as during small-group and whole-class instruction, during independent reading time, or in the classroom library. What exactly can you observe? Some suggestions include:

- oral language ability
- attitudes
- choices during "free time"
- specific behaviors related to print
- interests
- book-handling behaviors
- peer relationships

Ask yourself questions such as the following when observing a student's behaviors related to print:

- **When the student reads or works with print, does he or she approach the task confidently?**
- **Does the student have a strategy for attempting unfamiliar words in reading and writing?**
- **Does the student read and write for different purposes?**
- **Can the student retell what he or she reads in a logical order?**
- **Does the student select reading materials suited to his or her personal interests?**
- **Does the student select reading materials suited to his or her level of reading development?**

Answers to these kinds of questions will help you make instructional decisions and set goals for an individual student, and will help the student progress in learning.

Make your observations systematic rather than random. Decide whom to focus on. Select one student or several at a time to closely watch. Keep a record for each student, noting what you see by recording it on self-adhesive stickies or peel-off labels that can be attached to the student's personal folder. Alternatively, keep a class list for easy referral.

When behaviors are observed, a check (✓) may be used. You may also wish to make a slash (/) the first time the behavior is observed and convert the slash to an X when you feel the behavior is performed with frequency. Indicating dates is helpful.

Decide when to observe. Observe during a time students are normally using books, when they first come into the room in the morning, or during a time they are involved in various learning centers. You may need to initiate the experience with students who do not independently go to books. Collect pertinent data, including written work samples and recordings of oral reading, and keep anecdotal records. Speak with parents for additional input.

ASSESSMENT
RUNNING RECORDS

An effective reader uses the visual information, based on knowledge of language and the content, to predict what comes next in the text, to check this prediction by taking in new visual information or by thinking about whether the prediction makes sense, and to confirm or reject this prediction in the light of this new information. If the prediction is rejected, the reader self-corrects.

When a student reads aloud, you can record what is read and look more closely at what the student is thinking and doing. Oral reading miscues reveal a student's reading strategies. Any miscues can be analyzed to make teaching decisions about the suitability of the level of the guided reading books being read and about the type of help a student may need. One way of doing this is to take a running record of oral reading.

Using a Running Record
Follow this assessment procedure to periodically monitor reading strategies:

First Step	Select something that is known to the student for him or her to read orally. (If it is too familiar, the reading may not reveal much information about the child's thinking.) This may be: • **a guided reading book,** • **a poem,** • **a dictated piece of the child's writing,** • **some of the student's published personal writing.**
Second Step	Ask the student to read the selected piece aloud. Record the student's reading in one of these ways: • **Record the correct reading and miscues on a blank piece of paper as the student reads, keeping the same linear arrangement of the text.** **OR** • **Make a copy of the text and mark the miscues on it as the student reads.**
Third Step	Tabulate the miscues. Use symbols to indicate what the student is doing. Some usual conventions follow.

Accurate reading	✓ ✓ ✓	(checks follow text pattern)
Substitution	wet *(child)* / Went *(text)*	
Attempt	w-we-wet / went	
Self-correction	wet / Went SC	
Omission	- / went	(or circle word)
Insertion	is / went	(or use carat)
Teacher told	- / Went T	(or underline word)
Repetition (of word or sentence)	R2 (numeral indicated number of repeats)	(or wavy underlines)

Evaluation: Analysis of the Running Record

Miscues in oral reading performance help you to identify the strategies a student uses. Ask yourself why the student makes each error. To determine what cues the student depends on, consider the following:

- **Does the student use visual cues from letters and words, such as *they* for *them*?**
- **Does the student use context clues to construct meaning? Inaccurate reading that makes sense indicates the student is probably using prior knowledge or familiar oral language.**
- **Does the student use knowledge of the grammatical structure of language? Again, the student's own oral language may influence a response.**

Make your best guess as to what cues the student uses, recording by the miscues *v* for visual cues, *m* for meaning, and *s* for structure. One or more types of cues might be used for any miscue. By analyzing each miscue in this way you can get an indication of the strategies the student is using, as well as those not being used or those being overused. Also notice instances of self-correction. Self-correction is an important skill in good reading.

Finally, make any notes on the running record about behaviors during the session. All of this information will assist you in assessing the student.

Running Records as a Regular Monitoring Tool

For each student who is able to read some type of continuous text, it is useful to take a running record about every six weeks. Repeat more often for students for whom you have concerns. For fluent readers it would only be necessary at the beginning, middle, and end of the school year.

Establish a system. For example, you might choose one student per school day, keeping the dated record and analysis in each student's portfolio to monitor the progress during the year. Select a time when you can hear the student read without interruptions, such as when other students are engaged in individual quiet reading.

Sample Running Record

Name: _____ Date: _____

Title: _____

PAGE	TEXT INFORMATION USED	RUNNING RECORD	
4	The animals had a picnic	✓ ✓ have ✓ ✓	v, m
	To celebrate the fair.	✓ ✓ ✓ ✓	
	They all brought something tasty	✓ ✓ bought ✓ t/testy/SC	v, m, s
	For everyone to share.	✓ ✓ ✓ ✓	
7	The lambs brought yams.	✓ ✓ bought ✓	v, m, s
	The bees brought peas.	✓ ✓ bought ✓	v, m, s
	The poodles brought noodles	✓ ✓ bought ✓	v, m, s
	All sprinkled with cheese.	✓ sprin/sprinkle/SC ✓	
8	The cheetahs brought pitas.	✓ ✓ bought pasta/T	v, m, s
	The mice brought rice.	✓ ✓ bought ✓	v, m, s
	The moose brought juice	✓ ✓ bought ✓	v, m, s
	And a bucket of ice.	✓ ✓ ✓ ✓ ✓	
11	The pigs brought figs.	✓ ✓ bought ✓	v, m, s
	The bears brought pears.	✓ ✓ bought ✓	v, m, s
	The apes brought grapes	✓ ✓ bought ✓	v, m, s
	And some picnic chairs.	✓ ✓ ✓ ✓	
12	The raccoons brought spoons.	✓ ✓ ✓ ✓	
	The moles brought bowls.	✓ ✓ ✓ ✓	
	The storks brought forks	✓ ✓ ✓ fo/fork/SC	
	And some cinnamon rolls.	✓ ✓ c/cam/camon/T	v
15	The snakes brought cakes	✓ snake bought ✓	v, m, s
	And I brought the tea.	✓ ✓ ✓ ✓ ✓	
	It was a wild picnic –	✓ ✓ ✓ ✓ ✓	
	Just the animals and me!	✓ ✓ ✓ ✓ ✓	

v=visual, m=meaning, s=structure

Teacher's Notes

Adib said, He told the story (pointing to picture) because it said,
"I brought the tea."
If bought *is counted as only one error, errors* $= \dfrac{103}{16} = 6.4$

Accuracy = 95%
Self-correction rate $= \dfrac{5 + 3}{3} = 2.6$

If each time brought *is read as an error; errors* $= \dfrac{100}{16} = 6.25$

Accuracy = 85%
Self-correction $= \dfrac{16 + 3}{3} = 6.33$

Adib is using all strategies when reading and seems to have cross-checked
one cue against another to self-correct. I could draw his attention to the
difference between brought *and* bought. *This book is at a suitable level of*
difficulty for instruction.

Evaluation of Suitability of Books

If a student is reading at an appropriate instructional level, approximately
94% of the text should be read accurately. An attempt at a word that is
eventually correct is not an error; record this as a self-correction and tally it as
accurately read. By calculating the percentage of accurately read words and
analyzing the types of errors, you'll be able to determine whether the student
is reading books at the appropriate instructional level, and you'll be able to
choose the right Guided Reading books for individuals and groups.

Students may select a guided reading book to have it read to them or to read
with a partner. In these instances the book may be easier or harder than the
instructional level.

ASSESSING AND BUILDING
READING FLUENCY

adapted from *Building Fluency* (Blevins, 2001)

> A large study conducted by the National Assessment of Educational Progress (Pinnell et al., 1995) concluded that 44 percent of fourth graders lacked the fluency levels necessary for grade level comprehension.
>
> The National Research Council report, *Preventing Reading Difficulties in Young Children* (Snow, Burns, and Griffin, 1998), states "Adequate progress in learning to read English (or, any alphabetic language) beyond the initial level depends on sufficient practice in reading to achieve fluency with different texts." The report recommends, "Because the ability to obtain meaning from print depends so strongly on the development of word recognition accuracy and reading fluency, both the latter should be regularly assessed in the classroom, permitting timely and effective instructional response when difficulty or delay is apparent."

Definition

Fluency is "the ability to read smoothly, easily, and readily with freedom from word recognition problems." (*A Dictionary of Reading and Related Terms*, Harris and Hodges, 1981) In order to help students develop fluency, you must first know their oral reading accuracy and rate. There are several measurement tools you can use to identify the accuracy and rate, and nationally-normed averages exist. Many state standards now include these rates as benchmarks of students' reading progress. The combination of reading accuracy and rate is referred to as a student's oral reading fluency (ORF). It is expressed as "words correct per minute" (WCPM).

It is essential to measure both accuracy and rate. For example, if you measure only accuracy, you wouldn't know that it takes one student twice as long to read the same text as it does another student. Which student is fluent? Likewise, if you measure only rate, you wouldn't know that one student, who could read a text much more quickly than another student, makes significantly more mistakes. Which student is fluent?

Measuring Reading Rate

To determine a student's oral reading rate, take a one-minute, timed sampling of his oral reading of a passage at his reading level. The passage must be unfamiliar to the student, can be taken from any grade-level textbook or book series, and must contain a minimum of 200 words. Make a copy of the passage for the student and one for yourself so you can record his errors while he reads. As the student reads, follow along and mark on your copy any words he reads incorrectly. Use the guidelines below. For example, if a student stops or struggles with a word for three seconds, tell him the word and mark it as incorrect. Place a mark after the last word he reads. Then, tally the results and consult the chart on the following pages, which shows national norms for oral reading rates of students in grades 2–8. Using these norms you can determine how your students rate nationally and which students need more work in developing fluency.

Note: Some educators suggest using three passages to avoid the content of any one passage affecting the fluency score. Have the student read each passage for one minute, noting all three scores. The median (middle) score is the student's fluency score for that testing period. For example, if a student scores 100, 102, and 110, his fluency score is 102. Use the same three passages for testing in the fall, winter, and spring.

Oral Reading Fluency Test-Scoring Guidelines

1. Words Read Correctly

These are words that the student pronounces correctly, given the reading context.
- Count self-corrections within 3 seconds as correct.
- Don't count repetitions as incorrect.

2. Words Read Incorrectly

Count the following types of errors as incorrect: (a) mispronunciations, (b) substitutions, and (c) omissions. Also, count words the student doesn't read within 3 seconds as incorrect.

- Mispronunciations are words that are misread: *bell* for *ball*.

- Substitutions are words that are substituted for the correct word; this is often inferred by a one-to-one correspondence between word orders: *dog* for *cat*.
- Omissions are words skipped or not read; if a student skips an entire line, each word is counted as an error.

3. 3-second Rule

If a student is struggling to pronounce a word or hesitates for 3 seconds, tell the student the word, and count it as an error.

Oral Reading Fluency Norms Grades 2–5

(Hansbrouck, J.E. and G. Tindal, 1992)

Grade	Percentile	WCPM* Fall	WCPM Winter	WCPM Spring
2	75%	82	106	124
	50%	53	78	94
	25%	23	46	65
3	75%	107	123	142
	50%	79	93	114
	25%	65	70	87
4	75%	125	133	143
	50%	99	112	118
	25%	72	89	92
5	75%	126	143	151
	50%	105	118	128
	25%	77	93	100

* WCPM = words correct per minute

Oral Reading Fluency Norms Grades 6–8

(Gary Germann, 2001)

Grade	Percentile	WCPM* Fall	WCPM Winter	WCPM Spring
6	90%	171	184	200
	75%	143	161	172
	50%	115	133	145
	25%	91	106	116
	10%	71	82	91
7	90%	200	206	212
	75%	174	182	193
	50%	148	158	167
	25%	124	133	145
	10%	104	115	124
8	90%	206	217	223
	75%	183	193	198
	50%	155	165	171
	25%	128	141	146
	10%	101	112	118

* WCPM = words correct per minute

**Current Oral Reading Fluency Norms for grades 1–8 can be found at *www.edformation.com*. These norms are updated in the fall, winter, and spring of each school year. Oral Reading Fluency (ORF) norms are available at the 90, 75, 50, 25, and 10 Percentiles. They are the results of an electronic aggregation of all students using Edformation's AIMSweb Benchmark Web-based software and Edformation's Standard Oral Reading Benchmark Passages. Questions can be directed to Edformation, Inc., 6420 Flying Cloud Drive, Suite 204, Eden Prairie, MN 55344. Call 952.944.1882 or fax 952.944.1884.

How to Interpret the Fluency Norms

These norms can be used to make classroom decisions including:

- Screening and determining student eligibility for intervention programs,
- Setting instructional goals and objectives,
- Placing students in instructional groups,
- Selecting appropriate reading materials for students,
- Monitoring academic progress of students,
- Reporting student progress to parents, and
- Making adjustments to or changes in reading instruction.

Reading Norm Charts

The norms are listed as percentile scores. For example, a percentile score of 65 means that 65% of students received fluency scores equal to or lower than the number indicated. Generally, students reading at the 50th percentile will have good comprehension of grade-level texts. Therefore, a fourth-grade student reading at 118 wcpm (50th percentile) would be expected to have at least adequate comprehension of grade-level text at the end of the year. A fourth grader who reads 143 wcpm (75th percentile) would be expected to have excellent comprehension of grade-level text at the end of the year. Those reading at 92 wcpm (25th percentile) would, however, be expected to have difficulty comprehending grade-level text.

Six Ways to Develop Fluency

Rasinski (1994) has identified six ways to build fluency.

Model Fluent Reading	Students need many opportunities to hear texts read aloud. This can include daily read-alouds, books on audiocasette, and books read by peers during book-sharing. While you read aloud to students, highlight particular aspects of fluency, such as how you read dialogue the way you think the character would say it or how you raise your voice at the end of a question sentence.
Provide Direct Instruction and Feedback	Direct instruction in fluency includes, but isn't limited to, independent reading practice, fluent reading modeling, and monitoring students' reading rates.
Provide Reader Support	Readers need to practice reading both orally and silently. Feedback during oral reading can aid in building fluency and attending to key aspects of fluency—speed, accuracy, and intonation. The most popular reader support techniques are echo reading, choral reading, partner reading, and reader's theater. In addition, books on audiocassette can be used.
Use Repeated Readings of One Text	Repeated readings, a popular technique developed by Samuels (1979), has long been recognized as an excellent way to help students achieve fluency. It has been shown to increase reading rate and accuracy and transfer to new texts. The student's reading is timed and feedback is given based on word accuracy and number of words read correctly per minute. The student then practices with the text until ready for another timed reading.
Cue Phrase Boundaries in Text	One of the characteristics of proficient readers is the ability to group words together in meaningful units. Students who are having trouble with comprehension may not be putting words together in meaningful phrases or chunks as they read. Their oral reading is characterized by choppy, word-by-word delivery that impedes comprehension. One way to help is the use of phrase-cued texts in which the natural boundaries are marked on the passage. Students practice with the marked passage, then read the same passage unmarked.
Provide Students With Easy Reading Materials	Students need an enormous amount of individualized reading practice in materials that are not too difficult. The materials should be at the student's independent or instructional level (above 90% word recognition), not at the student's frustration level. Provide time in class for students to read independently or with partners, and also assign books to read at home on a daily basis.

BENCHMARK BOOKS

Level	Benchmark Book
Level A	School
Level B	Kites
Level C	From Egg to Robin
Level D	Too Many Balloons
Level E	A Buzz Is Part of a Bee
Level F	I Am Fire
Level G	Dinosaurs
Level H	My Pigs
Level I	A Day With Firefighters
Level J	Looking at Maps and Globes
Level K	Our Flag
Level L	Animal Tracks
Level M	Buddy: The First Seeing Eye Dog
Level N	A Dinosaur Named Sue: The Find of the Century
Level O	Desert Life
Level P	Weather
Level Q	Exploring the Titanic
Level R	Journey to Ellis Island: How My Father Came to America
Level S	Salsa Stories
Level T	Sounder
Level U	First Ladies: Women Who Called The White House Home
Level V	Under Wraps
Level W	Dive! My Adventures in the Deep Frontier
Level X	Children of the Wild West
Level Y	Tales Mummies Tell
Level Z	Triumph on Everest: A Photobiography of Sir Edmund Hillary

READING LEVEL CORRELATIONS*

Grade Level (Basal)	Guided Reading Levels	DRA Levels	Success for All Levels	Reading Recovery Levels	Stages of Reading	Lexiles	DRP Text
Kindergarten	A B	A 1 2	1–3	1–2	Emergent		
Pre-Primer	C D E	3 4 6–8	4–25 25	3–8	Emergent/ Early	200–400	
Primer	F G	10 12	26–27	9–12	Early/ Transitional	200–400	
1st Grade	H I	14 16	38–48	13–17	Early/ Transitional	200–400	25–30
2nd Grade	J–K L–M	18–20 24–28	2.0	18–28	Transitional Fluency/ Extending	300–600	30–44
3rd Grade	N O–P	30 34–38	3.0	30–38	Fluency/ Extending	500–800	44–54
4th Grade	Q–R	40	4.0	40–42	Fluency/ Extending Advanced	600–900	46–55
5th Grade	S–V	44	—	44	Fluency/ Extending Advanced	700– 1000	49–57
6th Grade	W–Z	—	—	—	Advanced	800– 1050	51–60

*See **Text Gradient Chart** on the back of your materials folder. This chart identifies the overlapping level ranges for each grade in *The Scholastic Guided Reading Program*.

USING THE GUIDED READING PROGRAM

Characteristics of Text

The easiest books are included in Levels A and B. We suggest that children begin using Level A books for guided reading after they have listened to many stories and participated in shared reading. They should have some familiarity with print and understand that you read print and move from left to right in doing so. Children need not know all the letters of the alphabet and their sounds before reading Level A books.

Level A includes picture books without words, some with simple labels or captions, and some with up to five or six words, often on one line. In general, these books have clear, easy-to-read print with generous space between words. These simple formats enable young children to focus on print and reading from left to right, while gradually increasing their control over more words. Many of the books have high-frequency words and repeating language patterns. Print is presented in a variety of ways, which helps children become flexible readers from the start. In general, the books focus on topics that are familiar to most children. Books with more complex topics usually have fewer words and will require more of an introduction and teacher-child interaction to support understanding.

Behaviors to Notice and Support

	Child's Name						
Understands familiar concepts in stories and illustrations							
Differentiates print from pictures							
Holds the book and turns pages from left to right							
Reads words from left to right							
Begins to match word-by-word, pointing with one finger under words							
Locates both known and new words							
Remembers and uses language patterns							
Relates the book to his/her experience							

USING THE
GUIDED READING PROGRAM

LEVEL
B

Characteristics of Text

Level B books generally have simple story lines or a single idea. The print is easy-to-read with adequate space between words so that children can point to words as they read. Books at this level generally have one or two lines of print on a page, somewhat longer sentences, and a variety of punctuation.

There is direct correspondence between the text and pictures, and repeating patterns support the reader. Topics are generally familiar to most children. If more complex concepts are involved, the reading of the book will require teacher-child interaction to support understanding.

Behaviors to Notice and Support

	Child's Name						
Demonstrates control of left-to-right movement and return sweep							
Begins to control word-by-word matching across two lines of text, pointing with one finger							
Notices and interprets detail in pictures							
Talks about ideas in the text							
Remembers and uses language patterns in text							
Uses knowledge of high-frequency words to check on reading							
Uses word-by-word matching to check on reading							
Notices mismatches in meaning or language							
Uses visual information, such as the first letter of the word, to read known and new words							
Pays close attention to print							
Notices features of letters and words							
Begins to self-monitor, noticing mismatches in meaning or language							
Rereads to confirm or figure out new words							

USING THE
GUIDED READING PROGRAM

Characteristics of Text

Level C books have simple story lines and topics that are familiar to most children. Some may offer a new viewpoint on a familiar topic. Level C books generally have more words and lines of print than books at earlier levels. Print is clear and readable with adequate space between words. Most sentences are simple, but some have more complex structure, offering readers a challenge. While Level C books include some repeating language patterns, these are more complex and there is a shift to more varied patterns. Language patterns are more likely to change from page to page, so children cannot rely on them to make predictions and must pay closer attention to print. Level C books include many high-frequency words, as well as easily decodable words.

Behaviors to Notice and Support

	Child's Name						
Demonstrates control of left-to-right directionality and word-by-word matching across several lines of print							
Begins to track print with eyes							
Rereads to solve problems, such as figuring out new words							
Demonstrates awareness of punctuation by pausing and using some phrasing							
Uses picture details to help figure out words							
Remembers and uses language patterns in text							
Rereads to confirm or figure out new words							
Solves some new words independently							
Controls directionality and word-by-word matching with eyes, using finger at points of difficulty							
Uses visual information to predict, check, and confirm reading							
Recognizes known words quickly and uses them to figure out the meaning of new words							
Searches for understanding while reading							

USING THE
GUIDED READING PROGRAM

LEVEL
D

Characteristics of Text

Stories at Level D are slightly more complex than at previous levels. Generally, Level D books have topics that are familiar to most children, but also include some abstract or unfamiliar ideas. Text layout is still easy to follow with both large and small print. Sentences are a little longer than at Level C. Some are carried over to the next page or several pages and use a full range of punctuation. There are more compound words, multisyllable words, and words with a variety of inflectional endings. Illustrations are still supportive but less so than at the previous level, requiring the reader to pay more attention to print.

Behaviors to Notice and Support

	Child's Name							
Remembers language patterns and repeating events over longer stretches of text								
Self-corrects, using visual information								
Controls directionality and word-by-word matching with eyes, using finger only at points of difficulty								
Searches for understanding while reading								
Remembers details from the text and pictures								
Pays close attention to words and their structural features (for example, endings)								
Reads fluently, with phrasing								
Rereads to confirm or figure out new words								
Solves new words using knowledge of sound/letter relationships and word parts								

USING THE
GUIDED READING PROGRAM

Characteristics of Text

Level E books are generally longer than books at previous levels, either with more pages or more lines of text on a page. Some have sentences that carry over several pages and have a full range of punctuation. The text structure is generally more complex: stories have more or longer episodes, and informational books have more difficult ideas and concepts. However, in texts with more difficult concepts, there are usually repeating language patterns that offer some support. There are more multisyllable and compound words at this level.

Behaviors to Notice and Support

	Child's Name						
Tracks print with eyes except at points of difficulty							
Uses language syntax and meaning to read fluently, with phrasing							
Demonstrates awareness of punctuation by pausing, phrasing, and reading with inflection							
Rereads to self-monitor or self-correct phrasing and expression							
Recognizes many words quickly and automatically							
Figures out some longer words by taking them apart							
Relates texts to others previously read							
Reads for meaning but checks with the visual aspects of print (letters, sounds, words)							
Rereads to search for meaning and accuracy							
Remembers details and uses them to clarify meaning							
Demonstrates understanding by talking about text after reading							

USING THE
GUIDED READING PROGRAM

Characteristics of Text

In general, texts at Level F are longer and have more story episodes than at previous levels. There are also shorter texts with some unusual language patterns. Books have some concepts unfamiliar to children and some are even abstract, requiring reflection. Pictures continue to support reading, but closer attention to print is required. Language patterns are more characteristic of written language than of spoken language. Some Level F books have smaller print and more words and lines of text. There are many more new words and a greater variety of high-frequency words. A full range of punctuation is used to enhance meaning.

Behaviors to Notice and Support

	Child's Name							
Tracks print with eyes, using the hand only at points of difficulty								
Demonstrates awareness of punctuation by pausing, phrasing, and reading with inflection								
Uses syntax of written language to figure out new words and their meaning								
Uses sound/letter relationships, word parts, and other visual information to figure out new words								
Uses known words to figure out new words								
Uses multiple sources of information to search and self-correct								
Figures out longer words while reading for meaning								
Rereads to figure out words, self-correct, or improve phrasing and expression								
Rereads to search for meaning								
Recognizes most words quickly and automatically								
Moves quickly through the text								
Reads fluently, with phrasing								
Talks about ideas in the text and relates them to his/her experiences and to other texts								

USING THE
GUIDED READING PROGRAM

Characteristics of Text

Most books at Level G are not repetitive. These books include a variety of patterns. Knowledge of punctuation is important in understanding what the sentence means and how it should be spoken. Vocabulary is more challenging, with a greater range of words and more difficult words, including some that are technical and require content knowledge. Concepts and ideas may be less familiar than at previous levels. Level G books have a greater variety of styles of print and text layout, requiring close attention to print and flexibility on the part of the reader.

Behaviors to Notice and Support

	Child's Name						
Reads fluently and rapidly, with appropriate phrasing							
Follows print with eyes, occasionally using finger at points of difficulty							
Notices and uses punctuation to assist smooth reading							
Recognizes most words quickly and automatically							
Uses sound/letter relationships, known words, and word parts to figure out new words							
Uses meaning, visual information, and language syntax to figure out words							
Rereads to figure out words, self-correct, or improve phrasing and expression							
Rereads to search for meaning							
Remembers details to support the accumulation of meaning throughout the text							
Uses pictures for information but does not rely on them to make predictions							

USING THE
GUIDED READING PROGRAM

Characteristics of Text

Level H books are similar in difficulty to Level G, but Level H has a wider variety, including books with poetic or literary language. Sentences vary in length and difficulty, and some complex sentences carry over several pages. Children will need to be familiar with the syntactic patterns that occur. Books have fewer repeating events and language patterns, requiring more control of aspects of print. The vocabulary is expanded and includes words that are less frequently used in oral language. The size of print varies widely.

Behaviors to Notice and Support

	Child's Name							
Reads fluently and rapidly, with appropriate phrasing								
Follows the text with eyes, using finger only at points of particular difficulty								
Notices and uses punctuation to assist smooth reading								
Recognizes most words rapidly								
Uses sound/letter relationships, known words, and word parts to figure out new words								
Uses meaning, visual information, and language syntax to solve problems								
Rereads phrases to figure out words, self-correct, or improve phrasing and expression								
Rereads to search for meaning								
Remembers details to support meaning accumulated through the text								
Uses pictures for information but does not rely on them to make predictions								
Searches for meaning while reading, stopping to think or talk about ideas								

USING THE
GUIDED READING PROGRAM

Characteristics of Text

In general, the books at Level I are longer and more complex than at Levels G and H. The size of print is smaller and there are many more lines of print on the page. Books have longer sentences and paragraphs. There are more multisyllabic words, requiring complex word-solving skills. This level offers a greater variety of texts, including some that are informational, with technical language. Events in the text are more highly elaborated. Illustrations enhance the story, but provide low support for understanding meaning.

Behaviors to Notice and Support

	Child's Name						
Actively figures out new words using a range of strategies							
Follows the print with eyes							
Reads fluently, slowing down to figure out new words and then resuming speed							
Begins to silently read some of the text							
In oral reading, rereads some words or phrases to self-correct or improve expression							
Rereads to search for meaning							
Flexibly uses meaning, language syntax, and visual information to figure out new words and to monitor reading							
Self-corrects errors that cause loss of meaning							
Rereads when necessary to self-correct, but not as a habit							
Demonstrates understanding of the story and characters							
Goes beyond the text in discussions and interpretations							
Sustains problem-solving and development of meaning through a longer text and a two-or-three day period							

USING THE
GUIDED READING PROGRAM

Characteristics of Text

Although it supports essentially the same reading behaviors, Level J offers more difficult and varied books than Level I. It includes informational books with new concepts and beginning chapter books with complex narratives and memorable characters. The amount of print varies; some Level J books have full pages of text with few illustrations. Generally, illustrations enhance the text but offer little support for understanding text meaning or figuring out new words. The difficulty of the language also varies. There are books with easy and familiar language and others with literary language or other challenges. Texts have many high-frequency words but may also have unfamiliar and/or technical words.

Behaviors to Notice and Support

Child's Name								
Uses multiple sources of information to process text smoothly								
Uses multiple strategies to figure out new words while focusing on meaning								
Analyzes words from left to right, using knowledge of sound/letter relationships								
Uses known words and word parts to figure out new words								
Reads fluently, slowing down to figure out new words and then resuming speed								
Flexibly uses meaning, language syntax, and visual information to monitor reading								
Self-corrects errors that cause loss of meaning								
Rereads when necessary to self-correct, but not as a habit								
Rereads to search for meaning								
Demonstrates understanding of the story and characters								
Goes beyond the text in discussions and interpretations								
Sustains problem-solving and development of meaning through a longer text read over several days								
Silently reads sections of text								
Makes inferences, predicts, and analyzes character and plot								

USING THE
GUIDED READING PROGRAM

Characteristics of Text

The Level K collection includes longer chapter books with memorable characters, shorter informational books with technical language and new concepts, and literary texts with illustrations that enhance meaning. Stories have multiple episodes related to a single plot. Some stories have to do with times, places, and characters outside children's experience.

Readers will need to use a variety of strategies to figure out new writing styles. At this level, most reading will be silent, although teachers will always sample oral reading or invite children to read aloud for emphasis or enjoyment in group sessions. It will take more than one sitting for children to read some of the longer chapter books.

Behaviors to Notice and Support

	Child's Name						
Integrates multiple sources of information while reading with fluency							
When reading orally, reads rapidly, with phrasing, slowing down to problem solve and then resuming speed							
Reads silently much of the time							
Demonstrates understanding of the text after silent reading							
Makes inferences, predicts, and analyzes character and plot							
Flexibly uses multiple word-solving strategies while focusing on meaning							
Goes beyond the text in understanding of problems and characters							
Demonstrates facility in interpreting the text							
Sustains attention to meaning and interpretation of a longer text read over several days							

USING THE
GUIDED READING PROGRAM

Characteristics of Text

In general, reading behaviors for Level L are the same as for Level K except they are applied to longer and/or more complex books. At Level L there is greater variety of texts, including informational books, biographies, chapter books, and some longer, highly literary, or informational picture books.

Chapter books have more sophisticated plots and characters that are developed throughout the text. Some books have abstract or symbolic themes that require higher-level conceptual understandings. Texts contain an expanded vocabulary with many multisyllabic words.

Behaviors to Notice and Support

	Child's Name							
Integrates multiple sources of information while reading with fluency								
When reading orally, reads rapidly, with phrasing								
Reads orally, with accuracy, not stopping to self-correct in the interest of fluency and phrasing								
In oral reading, uses multiple word-solving strategies with longer words								
Reads silently most of the time								
Demonstrates understanding and facility in interpreting the text after silent reading								
After reading longer sections of a text, predicts events, outcomes, problem resolutions, and character changes								
Makes connections between the text read and other books								
Sustains attention to meaning and interpretation of a longer text read over several days								

USING THE
GUIDED READING PROGRAM

Characteristics of Text

Level M books have a variety of formats. Topics vary widely, and include subjects that will be familiar to children and those that are new. Literary selections have complex language and subtle meanings that require interpretation and background knowledge.

Chapter books are longer with few pictures. This requires readers to have mastery of the text. Many books have small print and little space between words. Vocabulary is expanded, and many words require background knowledge for comprehension.

Behaviors to Notice and Support

	Student's Name							
Uses multiple sources of information to figure out words rapidly while focusing on meaning								
Flexibly applies word-solving strategies to more complex, multisyllabic words								
Demonstrates facility in interpreting text while reading orally, with fluency and phrasing								
Reads orally with high accuracy in most instances, not stopping to self-correct errors in the interest of fluency and phrasing								
Reads silently, except during assessment or to demonstrate text interpretation								
After reading longer sections of text, predicts outcomes, problem resolutions, and character changes								
Remembers details and sustains attention to meaning through a longer text								
Demonstrates understanding and facility at interpretation after silent reading								
Makes connections between the text read and other books								
Goes beyond the text to make more sophisticated interpretations								

USING THE
GUIDED READING PROGRAM

Characteristics of Text

The Level N collection includes longer texts in a variety of genres. There are chapter books that present memorable characters developed through literary devices such as humor, irony, and whimsy. There are informational books and books that offer mystery and suspense. Level N also has shorter selections that provide opportunity to interpret texts and go beyond them. Vocabulary continues to expand, and topics go well beyond students' own experience.

Behaviors to Notice and Support

	Student's Name							
Uses multiple strategies to figure out new words quickly								
Demonstrates facility in text interpretation while reading orally, with fluency and phrasing								
Reads silently, except during assessment or when demonstrating text interpretation								
Remembers details from one section of text to the next								
Sustains attention to a longer text, remembering details and revising interpretations								
Notices how illustrations convey the author's meaning								
Demonstrates sophisticated interpretation of characters and plot								
Makes connections among a wide variety of texts								
Goes beyond the text to speculate on alternative meanings								

USING THE
GUIDED READING PROGRAM

Characteristics of Text

Books at Level O include selections from children's literature and chapter books. Books at this level explore more mature themes and topics that go beyond students' experience and expand it. Students can empathize with characters and learn about the lives of others. The vocabulary is sophisticated and varied. Most words will be known or within students' control; however, many will require interpretation of meaning. Many new multisyllabic words are included. Sentences are more complex and use a full range of punctuation.

Behaviors to Notice and Support

	Student's Name							
Solves words quickly and automatically while focusing on meaning								
Searches to understand the subtle shades of meaning that words can convey								
Demonstrates facility in text interpretation while reading orally, with fluency and phrasing								
In oral reading, figures out new words rapidly while reading smoothly and expressively								
Sustains attention to a text read over several days, remembering details and revising interpretations as new events are encountered								
After reading silently, demonstrates understanding and sophistication in text interpretation								
Makes connections among texts to enhance interpretation								
Goes beyond the text to speculate on alternative meanings								
Shows the ability to summarize the text in writing								

USING THE
GUIDED READING PROGRAM

Characteristics of Text

In general, books at this level are longer and ideas and language are more complex than at previous levels. Level P has a variety of informational texts, including history and biography. Through this variety, students become familiar with texts that are organized differently and learn how to gain information from them. Other genres include chapter books that explore the problems of early adolescents.

Behaviors to Notice and Support

Student's Name							
When reading silently, reads rapidly and with attention to meaning							
Actively acquires new vocabulary through reading							
Demonstrates facility in text interpretation while reading orally, with fluency and phrasing							
In oral reading, figures out new words rapidly while reading smoothly and expressively							
Sustains attention to a text read over many days, remembering details and revising interpretations as new events are encountered							
Demonstrates interest in reading an extended text over a longer time period							
After reading silently, demonstrates understanding and sophistication in interpreting meaning							
Compares the text with other books in an analytic way							
Goes beyond the text to speculate on alternative meanings							
Shows the ability to summarize and extend the text in writing							

LEVEL Q

USING THE GUIDED READING PROGRAM

Characteristics of Text

Level Q includes literature selections with sophisticated humor, complex plots, and memorable characters. Themes at this level are sophisticated and require interpretation. They serve as a good foundation for group discussion. Illustrations and their relationship to the text can be examined as well. Books have complex structure and difficult words that offer challenges. There are some words from languages other than English. Longer texts require an extended time period to read.

Behaviors to Notice and Support

	Student's Name							
Reads rapidly, with attention to meaning, when reading silently								
Actively acquires new vocabulary through reading								
Demonstrates facility in text interpretation while reading orally, with fluency and phrasing								
In oral reading, figures out new words rapidly while reading smoothly and expressively								
Sustains attention to a text read over many days, remembering details and revising interpretations as new events are encountered								
Demonstrates interest in reading an extended text over a longer time period								
Demonstrates interest in reading shorter literary texts								
Uses illustrations to help analyze text meaning								
After reading silently, demonstrates understanding and sophistication in interpreting meaning								
Compares the text to other books in an analytic way								
Goes beyond the text to speculate on alternative meanings								
Goes beyond the text to interpret characters' thoughts and feelings								
Shows the ability to analyze and extend the text in writing								

USING THE
GUIDED READING PROGRAM

Characteristics of Text

At Level R, both fiction and nonfiction have a range of historical place and time settings, giving students an opportunity to empathize with characters and learn about their lives and the times and places in which they lived. In general, skills are the same as at Level Q, but are extended over a wider variety of texts. Some books require sustained reading over a longer time period. Vocabulary and language are sophisticated and offer challenges to the reader.

Behaviors to Notice and Support

	Student's Name							
Reads rapidly, both orally and silently, while focusing on meaning								
Actively acquires new vocabulary while reading								
Sustains attention to a text read over many days, remembering details and revising interpretations as new events are encountered								
Demonstrates interest in reading an extended text over a longer time period								
Extends the text in various ways, including through research								
Demonstrates interest and ability in interpreting shorter selections								
Uses illustrations to help analyze text meaning								
After reading silently, demonstrates understanding and sophistication in interpreting meaning								
Uses comparison with other texts to assist interpretation								
Goes beyond the text to interpret characters' thoughts and feelings and to speculate on alternative meanings								
Demonstrates all interpretive and analytic skills in writing								

USING THE
GUIDED READING PROGRAM

Characteristics of Text

Level S includes literary selections, highly literary or informational picture books, and chapter books in a variety of genres. The collection reflects a wide variety of topics, cultures, and historical settings. Sentences and paragraphs at this level are complex.

Words present many shades of meaning which readers must interpret from the text and their own background knowledge. Selections offer opportunities for readers to make connections with other books they have read at earlier levels.

Behaviors to Notice and Support

	Student's Name						
Reads rapidly, both orally and silently, with attention to meaning							
Rapidly acquires new vocabulary through reading							
Sustains attention to a text read over many days, remembering details and revising interpretations as new events are encountered							
Demonstrates interest and ability in interpreting shorter selections							
Demonstrates flexibility in reading many different kinds of texts							
After reading silently, demonstrates understanding and sophistication in interpreting meaning							
Goes beyond the text to interpret characters' thoughts and feelings and to speculate on alternative meanings							
Demonstrates all analytic and interpretive skills in writing							
Extends text meaning through research, writing, or the arts							

USING THE
GUIDED READING PROGRAM

Characteristics of Text

The Level T collection has a great variety of genres. Short selections include informational books, legends, historical fiction, and folk tales. Chapter books include autobiographies, historical narratives, realistic fiction, science fiction, and other fantasy stories. Some chapter books are quite long and require reading over an extended time. Judgement is needed as to whether students can sustain interest for these longer selections. Selections contain many sophisticated, multisyllabic words, and readers will need to consider both their literal and connotative meanings.

Behaviors to Notice and Support

	Student's Name						
Reads rapidly, both orally and silently, with attention to meaning							
In oral and silent reading, figures out new words automatically and easily interprets word meaning							
Sustains attention to a text read over many days, remembering details and revising interpretations as new events are encountered							
Demonstrates interest and ability in interpreting shorter selections							
Demonstrates flexibility in reading texts of different styles and genres							
After reading silently, demonstrates understanding and ability to analyze characters and plot							
Reflects knowledge of literary genre in conversation and writing							
Extends and demonstrates understanding of the text through writing in a variety of genres							
Extends and demonstrates understanding of the text through public speaking, research, or the arts							

USING THE
GUIDED READING PROGRAM

Characteristics of Text

Texts at Level U require readers to employ a wide range of sophisticated reading strategies that approach adult levels. The difference, of course, is that elementary and middle school students are still gaining the world experience and content knowledge, or the accumulation of text experience needed to deeply understand the more complex texts they will be reading at levels U through Z. By this time, students have built an integrated processing system, but they need to apply their strategies to increasingly difficult levels of text. As they do so, reading with fluency and understanding, they will expand and build their reading strategies.

Fiction texts at level U may have several different themes and multiple story lines. Texts are increasingly literary, with writers expressing layers of meaning through symbolism. Themes are more abstract; creative formats may be used, such as collections of short stories that build meaning over different texts, or novels that incorporate diaries, poetry, or stories within stories. Generally, there are more characters to follow and their development is more complex; there are plots and subplots. Informational texts at Level U cover a wide range of topics and present specific, technical information. As with earlier levels, illustrations require interpretation and connection to text.

Behaviors to Notice and Support

	Student's Name						
Notices graphic illustrations and gets information from them							
Synthesizes information from graphic information with the body of the text							
Uses the table of contents to help in understanding the organization of the text							
Grasps "layers" of meaning in a story; for example, specific understandings plus the "bigger picture"							
Reads, understands, and appreciates literary language							
Interprets illustrations and their connections to the text							
Keeps up with several different themes and many characters							
Interprets characters' motives and the influences on their development							
Recognizes and appreciates a wide range of genres, both fiction and nonfiction							
Notices and uses a full range of punctuation, including more rarely used forms such as dashes							
Learns technical words from reading							
Uses reading to learn about self and others							

USING THE GUIDED READING PROGRAM

Characteristics of Text

At Level V, readers employ essentially the same range of strategies as at the previous level, but more background knowledge will be required for true understanding. Also, students will be rapidly adding to their reading vocabularies. Fiction includes science fiction that presents sophisticated ideas and concepts. In many works of realistic or historical fiction, the writer is conveying a significant message beyond the story. Readers must think critically and sustain attention, memory, and understanding of theme over much longer texts. Full appreciation of texts requires noticing aspects of the writer's craft, including metaphor, simile, and symbolism. Many long texts have print in a much smaller font.

Informational texts present complex ideas and may use more technical language. Topics are distant from students' experience in time and place. Biographies provide a significant amount of historical information. Many focus on harsh themes. Other longer biographies are told in narrative style but present complex themes.

Behaviors to Notice and Support

	Student's Name						
Understands and talks about complex themes, analyzing them and applying them to current life situations							
Understands many different perspectives that are encountered in fiction and nonfiction texts							
Evaluates both fiction and nonfiction texts for their authenticity and accuracy							
Deals with mature topics such as death, war, prejudice, and courage							
Thinks critically about and discusses the content of a literary work or the quality of writing							
Notices aspects of the writer's craft and looks at the text from a writer's point of view							
Sustains attention and thinking over the reading of texts that are long and have smaller fonts							
Tries new genres, topics, and authors, and is able to compare them with known genres, topics, and authors							
Makes connections across texts to notice an author's style or technique							
Understands symbolism in both realistic fiction and fantasy; discusses what symbols mean in terms of today's society							
Brings prior knowledge to bear in understanding literary references							
Learns technical language and concepts through reading							
Learns about self and others through reading, especially about societies that are different from one's own							

USING THE
GUIDED READING PROGRAM

Characteristics of Text

Texts at Level W have themes that explore the human condition, with the same kinds of social problems mentioned at earlier levels. Fiction and nonfiction texts present characters that suffer hardship and learn from it. The writing is sophisticated, with complex sentences, literary language, and symbolism. Texts vary in length; print is generally in a small font. Comprehending texts at this level will require awareness of social and political issues; through them, readers can learn to understand current social problems at deeper levels.

Fantasy includes science fiction as well as "high" fantasy that introduces heroic characters, questions, and contests between good and evil. Informational texts may present complex graphic information and require readers to possess a wide range of content knowledge and to understand all of the basic organizational structures for nonfiction. Narrative style biographies include many details of their subjects' lives and prompt readers to make inferences about what motivated their achievements.

Behaviors to Notice and Support

Student's Name							
Sustains reading over longer and more complex texts; is not intimidated by varying layouts and styles of print							
Builds understanding of a wide variety of human problems							
Uses reading to expand awareness of people who are different from oneself							
Understands and learns from characters' experiences							
Learns about self and others through reading; actively seeks understanding of people different from oneself by culture, period of history, or other variation							
Deals with mature themes such as prejudice, war, death, survival, and poverty, and is able to discuss them in relation to one's own experiences							
Understands the complexities of human characters as they develop and change; discusses one's own point of view and relationship to characters							
Integrates understandings derived from graphic illustrations and the text							
Expands world knowledge through reading							
Flexibly and automatically uses tools such as glossary, references index, credentials for authors, legends, charts, and diagrams							

USING THE
GUIDED READING PROGRAM

Characteristics of Text

Texts at Level X include the same wide range of genres shown at previous levels, but the themes explored are increasingly mature. High fantasy includes complex, extended symbolic narratives that require knowledge of previously-read texts for full understanding. Fantasy depicts quests and the struggle between good and evil. Readers are required to go substantially beyond the literal meaning of the text to construct a writer's implied meaning. In addition, texts require interpretation of theme and plot. In fiction texts, there may be many characters to follow and understand. There is a continuing increase in the sophistication of vocabulary, language, and topics. Nonfiction texts require extensive prior knowledge for full understanding. In addition, texts are designed to present a great deal of new knowledge, sometimes in a dense way. Graphic illustrations are helpful to readers but also require interpretation.

Behaviors to Notice and Support

	Student's Name							
Sustains attention over longer texts with more abstract, mature, and complex themes								
Notices, understands, and discusses a wide range of literary devices, such as flashbacks and stories within stories								
Deals with mature themes, such as family relationships, death, social injustice, and the supernatural								
Appreciates, understands, and discusses irony and satire								
Uses descriptive text as a way to understand settings and their importance to the plot or character development								
Discusses the setting as an element of the text, deciding whether it is important or unimportant								
Flexibly and automatically uses tools such as glossary, references index, credentials for authors, legends, charts, and diagrams								
Notices aspects of the author's craft, including the way characters are described and presented as "real"								
Talks about the text in an analytic way, including finding specific evidence of the author's style								
Understands and is able to use the sophisticated, scholarly, and technical language that is found in informational texts								

USING THE
GUIDED READING PROGRAM

Characteristics of Text

Books categorized as Level Y present subtle themes and complex plots. As with earlier levels, they include a whole range of social problems as themes, but more explicit details (for example, about death or prejudice) may be provided. Readers will need to bring considerable world experience and reading experience to their understanding of these more mature texts. Writers use symbolism, irony, satire, and other literary devices that require readers to think beyond the literal meaning of the text.

Books at Level Y include many more complex works of fantasy that depict hero figures and heroic journeys. Readers are required to discern underlying lessons and also to analyze texts for traditional elements. Informational texts explore an ever-widening world of history and science; topics require extensive prior knowledge of complex concepts, as well as vocabulary. Readers are required to gather new information from reading and synthesize it with their current knowledge. A wide range of critical reading skills are also required, so that students continuously evaluate the quality and objectivity of the texts they read.

Behaviors to Notice and Support

	Student's Name						
Understands and discusses subtle and complex plots and themes							
Understands, discusses, and deals with, in a mature way, a wide range of social problems, including social injustice and tragedy							
Understands and discusses in a mature way texts that present explicit details of social problems							
Understands literary irony and satire as they are used to communicate big ideas							
Understands complex fantasy, entering into whole new worlds, and understands concepts in relation to the imagined setting							
Understands and discusses the fact that words can have multiple meanings in relation to the context in which they are used							
Flexibly and automatically uses tools such as glossary, references index, credentials for authors, legends, charts, and diagrams							
Interprets events in the light of the setting—time, place, and culture							
Engages in critical thinking about fiction and nonfiction texts							
Critically evaluates nonfiction texts for accuracy and presentation of information							

USING THE GUIDED READING PROGRAM

Characteristics of Text

Level Z captures books that require reading strategies similar to those needed at lower levels, but which present such mature themes that readers simply need more experience to deal with them. Some students who are widely read may need this challenge. Some informational books present complex and technical information, sometimes within a denser text. Others deal with controversial social concepts and political issues that require readers to evaluate several points of view. Critical reading is essential, and readers often have to re-evaluate and revise their own previously held beliefs. Historical texts have detailed accounts of periods of history that are less well known. Readers learn new ways of finding technical information, and encounter complex examples of the basic organizational structures for informational texts. Fiction texts explore a wide range of human themes, often with graphic details of hardship, violence, or tragedy. High fantasy presents heroic quests, symbolism, and complex characters, and involves the reader in considering the meaning of life.

Behaviors to Notice and Support

	Student's Name							
Sustains reading and understanding over much longer texts								
Deals with a great range of texts—from diaries to narratives to plays								
Switches easily from one genre to another, accessing knowledge of the structure and nature of the text while beginning to read								
Understands and discusses how a text "works" in terms of the writer's organization								
Deals with controversial social and political issues, seeing multiple perspectives								
Uses reading to gain technical knowledge in a wide variety of areas								
Understands the symbolism in heroic quests; applies concepts encountered in fantasy to today's life								
Flexibly and automatically uses tools such as glossary, references index, credentials for authors, legends, charts, and diagrams								
Deals with and discusses in a mature way graphic details such as accounts of brutality, hardship, or violence								
Notices, understands, appreciates, and discusses literary devices								
Understands and appreciates complex language, archaic language, and cultural motifs								
Learns about epilogues, bibliographies, and forewords								
Builds information across the text, even when very unusual formats are used (for example, brief interviews with many characters)								
Fully understands the subtle differences between fiction and nonfiction								

READING LOG

	Child's Name								
Level A									
Big and Little									
Games									
I Can, We Can									
In the Woods									
Kittens									
Let's Go!									
My Color									
School									
We Can!									
What Bears Like									
Level B									
Baby Animals Learn									
Carrots									
Goldilocks									
Hop In!									
Kites									
Two Can Do It!									
Water									
We Are Painting									
We Like to Play!									
What Am I?									
Level C									
At Work									
Bugs!									
From Egg to Robin									
How Many Can Play?									
I Can Run									
I See Fish									
It's a Party									
Joshua James Likes Trucks									
Pancakes, Crackers, and Pizza									
Rain									

READING LOG

	Child's Name								
Level D									
Footprints in the Snow									
I Know Karate									
Nests, Nests, Nests									
One Happy Classroom									
Paul the Pitcher									
Rain! Rain!									
Ten Cats Have Hats									
Too Many Balloons									
Where Do Birds Live?									
Who Am I?									
Level E									
Animal Babies									
A Box Can Be Many Things									
A Buzz Is Part of a Bee									
Clay Art									
I Can See									
Just Like Me									
Look! I Can Read!									
Polar Babies									
Up, Up, and Away									
The Voyage of Mae Jemison									
Level F									
Amy Loves the Snow									
Cookie's Week									
Firehouse Sal									
Frog's Lunch									
Harry's House									
I Am Fire									
Is This You?									
Pizza Party!									
Shine, Sun!									
Soccer Game!									

READING LOG

	Child's Name								
Level G									
The Class Trip									
Dinosaurs									
The Great Race									
Make It Move!									
Pelé: The King of Soccer									
Sam the Garbage Hound									
Sometimes Things Change									
Teddy Bear For Sale									
Wait, Skates!									
Why Can't I Fly?									
Level H									
Caps, Hats, Socks, and Mittens									
Come! Sit! Speak!									
Danny and the Dinosaur Go to Camp									
It's Spring!									
A Kiss for Little Bear									
My Pigs									
Plane Rides									
The Very Big Potato									
What Will the Weather Be Like Today?									
When I First Came to This Land									
Level I									
All Tutus Should Be Pink									
A Day with a Mail Carrier									
A Day with Firefighters									
The Elves and the Shoemaker									
Goldilocks and the Three Bears									
I Am a Rock									
Messy Bessey's Family Reunion									
Red-Eyed Tree Frog									
The Sun's Family of Planets									
We Just Moved!									

READING LOG

	Child's Name								

Level J

Bear Shadow									
Henry and Mudge and the Long Weekend									
How Kittens Grow									
Jack Plays the Violin									
Looking at Maps and Globes									
Me on the Map									
My Life									
On the Lake									
Poppleton Everyday									
The Sword in the Stone									

Level K

All About Things People Do									
The Blue Mittens									
Chickens Aren't the Only Ones									
The Day Jimmy's Boa Ate the Wash									
Ming Lo Moves the Mountain									
Our Flag									
Penguins									
A Place for Grace									
Shipwreck Saturday									
What Magnets Can Do									

Level L

Animal Tracks									
Apatosaurus									
The Big "M"									
Cam Jansen and the Mystery of the Babe Ruth Baseball									
The Mud Pony									
Play Ball, Amelia Bedelia									
Rain Forest									
Solve It!									
Spiders									
This Is My House									

READING LOG

	Student's Name								
Level M									
At 1600 Pennsylvania Avenue									
Boom!									
Buddy: The First Seeing Eye Dog									
California or Bust!									
Firefighters									
Gung Hay Fat Choy									
Jungle Jack Hanna's Safari Adventure									
The Littles Go Exploring									
Nine True Dolphin Stories									
Yellowstone National Park									
Level N									
Amber Brown Is Feeling Blue									
Catwings Return									
The Corn Husk Doll									
A Dinosaur Named Sue									
Do Tornadoes Really Twist?									
Endangered Animals									
The Garden on Green Street									
How Is a Crayon Made?									
Lily and Miss Liberty									
Louis Braille: The Boy Who Invented Books for the Blind									
Level O									
The Animal Shelter Mystery									
Desert Life									
Donner Party									
Flossie & the Fox									
I Wonder Why Snakes Shed Their Skins									
The Kids' Invention Book									
Look What Came from Mexico									
Miss Rumphius									
A Picture Book of Sojourner Truth									
Where There Was Smoke									

READING LOG

Student's Name

Level P

26 Fairmount Avenue								
The Drum Beats On								
The Eagle Has Landed								
Encyclopedia Brown Carries On								
In the Rain Forest								
The Magic School Bus: Inside a Beehive								
The Real McCoy								
Shoebag								
Weather								
A Whale Is Not a Fish and Other Animal Mix-ups								

Level Q

Adventures of the Shark Lady								
American Tall Tales								
Animals of Long Ago								
Exploring the Titanic								
Favorite Medieval Tales								
Folktales from China								
Help! I'm Trapped in the First Day of Summer Camp								
...If You Lived With the Cherokee								
Mary on Horseback								
Native American Art								

Level R

And Then What Happened, Paul Revere?								
Brian's Winter								
Draw Me a Story								
A Jar of Dreams								
Journey to Ellis Island								
The Last Princess								
Lewis and Clark: In Their Own Words								
Listening to Crickets								
Pigs Might Fly								
The Tortoise Shell & Other African Stories								

READING LOG

Student's Name

Level S

Ben and Me									
Bessie Coleman									
The Broccoli Tapes									
The Chicago Fire									
Earthquake! A Story of Old San Francisco									
Eureka! It's Television!									
In the Line of Fire: Eight Women War Spies									
In the Year of the Boar and Jackie Robinson									
Salsa Stories									
The Star Fisher									

Level T

The Big Lie: A True Story									
The Girl Who Chased Away Sorrow									
Bonanza Girl									
Sleepers, Wake									
Sounder									
The Story of Levi's									
The Tall Tale of John Henry									
Under the Royal Palms									
Volcano: The Eruption and Healing of Mount St. Helens									
Where Are the Wolves?									

Level U

First Ladies: Women Who Called the White House Home									
Geysers: When Earth Roars									
Golden Games									
Great Explorations									
Hoang Anh									
An Indian Winter									
Midnight Magic									
The Secret Garden									
Sir Arthur									
The Story of My Life									

READING LOG

Level V

	Student's Name								
1000 Facts About Space									
Alice In Wonderland									
Eleanor Roosevelt									
Get on Board									
Harry Potter and the Chamber of Secrets									
How I Came to Be a Writer									
The Music of Dolphins									
Old Yeller									
The True Confessions of Charlotte Doyle									
Under Wraps									

Level W

Buried In Ice									
Dive!									
The First Woman Doctor									
From Rags to Riches									
The Moon Bridge									
Our World of Mysteries									
The Phantom Tollbooth									
Sea Otter Rescues									
Through My Eyes									
You Want Women to Vote, Lizzie Stanton?									

Level X

Anne Frank: Beyond the Diary									
At Her Majesty's Request									
Bully for You, Teddy Roosevelt!									
Call It Courage									
Children of the Wild West									
M.C. Higgins the Great									
One More River to Cross									
Out of the Dust									
Sarah Bishop									
Summer of Fire									

READING LOG

Student's Name

Level Y

Blizzard!									
Castle									
The Colorado River									
The Day Martin Luther King, Jr. Was Shot									
I Am an American									
My Brother Sam Is Dead									
Restless Spirit									
Seeing Earth From Space									
Tales Mummies Tell									
Usborne Tales of Real Escape									

Level Z

Black Beauty									
City: A Story of Roman Planning and Construction									
The Day Women Got the Vote									
Great Escapes of World War II									
The History of Emigration from China & Southeast Asia									
The Adventures of Tom Sawyer									
Treasure Island									
Triumph on Everest									
We Shall Not Be Moved									
Where the River Runs									

EVALUATION RESPONSE FOR TEXT GRADIENT

adapted from *Guided Reading: Good First Teaching for All Children* (Fountas and Pinnell, 1996)

Directions: Since any gradient is always in the process of construction when it is used with varying groups of students, we expect our list to change every year. We encourage you to try the levels with your students and to provide feedback based on your own experiences. Please suggest changes to existing book levels and suggest new books for the list. Please provide the information requested.

Name: _____ **Grade Level You Teach:** _____

Telephone: _____ **Email Address:** _____

Address: _____

Book Evaluated

Book Title: _____ **Level:** _____

Author: _____ **Publisher:** _____

This book is

_____ A book that I have evaluated by using it with my class.

To what level should it be moved? _____

Why? _____

_____

_____ A book that I am recommending as a benchmark book.

How does it support readers at this level? _____

What challenge does it offer? _____

_____

_____ A new book that I am recommending to the collection.

To what level should it be placed? _____

Why? _____

_____

Copy and mail this form to:
Gay Su Pinnell
The Ohio State University
200 Ramseyer Hall
29 W. Woodruff Avenue
Columbus, OH 43210

ADDITIONAL LEVELED BOOKS
AVAILABLE FROM SCHOLASTIC

Level A

Dogs
Toys Night Out
Have You Seen My Duckling?
Time to Get Up!
I Am
Games
I Can, Too!
I Like
Legs
Lunch
My Cats
We Like Fruit
What Do Insects Do?

Level B

Hats Around the World
On Market Street
How Many Fish?
Have You Seen My Duckling?
I Like Shapes
All My Little Ducklings
In the Forest
We Work Together
Lunch at the Zoo
Pop
Making Mountains
Monkeys
My Cat Muffin
Who Lives in the Arctic?
Who Lives in Trees?

Level C

Bo and Peter
Jim and the Beanstalk
Boots
A World of Animals

In the City
I Went Walking
Is It Time to Go?
At the Park
Little Sister
Teddy Bear, Teddy Bear
One For You, One For Me
I Can Draw
Raindrops
Run, Run, Run
Swing, Swing, Swing
Water
Weather
Lots of Oranges
What Has Stripes?
A Bat and a Rat

Level D

The Ball Game
My Messy Room
Don't Be Late!
I See It
The Haircut
Bear in a Square
Hide and Seek
Two Crazy Pigs
I Love Mud and Mud Loves Me
Wake Up, Wake Up
I'm Hungry
I See a Bug
Making a Memory
School Bus
Not Enough Water
Two Eyes, a Nose, and a Mouth
What Is Big?
Winter Is Here!

Level E

Collections
A Bad, Bad Day
A Funny Man
Cat's Colors
Is Tomorrow My Birthday?
Coco Can't Wait!
Just a Seed
I Am Water
My Dad's Truck
Is it Dark? Is it Light?
Paper Bag Trail
Herman the Helper
Tortillas
Eat Your Peas, Louise!
A Tree Can Be...
Millions of Snowflakes
Wake Me in Spring
One Snowy Day
Which Hat Today?
Amy Loves the Rain

Level F

Beautiful Bugs
A Bug, a Bear, and a Boy
Bread, Bread, Bread
A Color of His Own
How Far Will I Fly?
Across the Stream
Itchy, Itchy Chicken Pox
Mama Cat Has Three Kittens
Messages
Five Little Ducks
Monkey See, Monkey Do
Ten Black Dots
Monster Math Picnic
Rosie's Walk

My Dog's the Best!
Mouse Count
Shoveling Snow
Amy Loves the Wind
"What Is That?" Said the Cat
Time to…

Level G

All About You
Each Peach Pear Plum
Buzz Said the Bee
City Sounds
Sunflower Seeds
How Have I Grown?
All About You
I Shop With My Daddy
Catch the Ball!
I'm a Caterpillar
My Friends
Monster Math School Time
One Monday Morning
My Friends
Ten, Nine, Eight
Say It, Sign It
Snow? Let's Go!
Who Stole the Cookies From
   the Cookie Jar?
Zoo-Looking

Level H

A Clean House for Mole and
Mouse
What Time Is It?
The Dinosaur Who lived
   In My Backyard
Water
George Shrinks
A Day With Firefighters

I Was Walking Down the Road
Dinosaur Roar!
Mom's Secret
A Big Fat Enormous Lie
More Spaghetti, I Say!
I Love Spiders
Mr. McCready's Cleaning Day
The Seasons of Arnold's Apple Tree
The New Baby Calf
The Shape of Things
Robert and the Rocket
Time to Sleep
Whose Mouse Are You?
Cows Can't Fly

Level I

Amalia and the Grasshopper
Alligators All Around
Apples and Pumpkins
Boom Boom Boom
The Gingerbread Man
A Mouse Told His Mother
Henny Penny
Froggy Goes to School
The Little Mouse, the Red
   Ripe Strawberry, and the
   Big Hungry Bear
How I Spent My Summer Vacation
Look-Alike Animals
The Camera
My Father
I'm Going to Be a Farmer
Noisy Nora
Leo the Late Bloomer
This Is the Place for Me
McDuff Moves In
Too Many Puppies
Seven Blind Mice

Level J

Bear's Bargain
Owl at Home
Big Mama and Grandma Ghana
Curious George Takes a Job
City Mouse—Country Mouse
Elephants Swim
Fox and His Friends
Germs! Germs! Germs!
Insects
Panda's Surprise
The Magic Fish
In the Forest
Mouse Soup
Inch by Inch
Mr. Putter and Tabby Walk the Dog
Officer Buckle and Gloria
Pack 109
Sun Up, Sun Down
Stone Soup
One of Each

Level K

Bedtime for Frances
Bats
The Blind Men and the Elephant
Zomo the Rabbit
The Bremen-town Musicians
All About Things People Do
Clifford the Big Red Dog
Chester's Way
Frog and Toad Are Friends
Caps for Sale
Jamaica's Find
A Birthday for Frances
Keep the Lights Burning, Abbie
Ruby the Copycat

Little Polar Bear and the Brave
Little Hare
Big Bob and the Magic
   Valentine's Day Potatoes
Martin and the Tooth Fairy
How Much is a Million?
Nathan and Nicholas Alexander
The Music Teacher from
   the Black Lagoon

Level L

Alexander and the
   Wind-Up Mouse
Alone in His Teacher's House
Big Al
Anansi and the Spider
Happy Birthday,
   Martin Luther King
Antarctica
Harry and Willy and Carrothead
Crow Boy
How Much Is That Guinea Pig
   in the Window?
The Fly on the Ceiling
Katy and the Big Snow
Heckedy Peg
The Littles
Hill of Fire
The Puppy Who Wanted a Boy
Horrible Harry and the Green Slime
The Schoolyard Mystery
The Baby-sitters Club
Baby Tamer
Duke Ellington

Level M

Black Bear Cub
Abe Lincoln's Hat

A Book About Your Skeleton
Angel Child, Dragon Child
Boundless Grace
Mighty Spiders
Cam Jansen and the Mystery
   of the U.F.O.
Doctor De Soto
A Chair for My Mother
Fables
Cloudy With a Chance
   of Meatballs
Follow the Drinking Gourd
Five True Dog Stories
Tar Beach
George Washington's Mother
The Reason for a Flower
The Popcorn Book
The Emperor's Egg
What Zookeepers Do
The Girl Who Loved Wild Horses

Level N

Amber Brown Is Not a Crayon
Stellaluna
The Cat Who Wore a Pot
   on Her Head
Fire Fighters
The Cat's Meow
From Seed to Plant
Dolphin's First Day
Most Wonderful Doll in the World
Horrible Harry and
   the Ant Invasion
Johnny Appleseed
Mummies in the Morning: Magic
Tree House #3
Why Mosquitoes Buzz
   in People's Ears

Rumplestiltskin
Lion Dancer
We'll Never Forget You, Roberto
Clemente
Shark Lady
What Am I Made Of?
Dare to Dream

Level O

Borreguita and the Coyote:
A Tale from Ayutla, Mexico
A New Coat for Anna
The Boxcar Children #1
A Picture Book of
   Benjamin Franklin
Case of the Secret Message:
   Clue Jr. #1
Eleanor
City Green
Ten True Animal Rescues
Elaine and the Flying Frog
The Magic School Bus Hops Home
The Hundred Dresses
Ant Cities
The Legend of the Blue Bonnet
Creatures That Glow
Owl Moon
Paul Bunyan
The Spray-Paint Mystery
They Led the Way
The Story of Ruby Bridges
The Mud Pony

Level P

Circle of Gold
Amelia and Eleanor Go For a Ride
Ghost Versus Ghost: BB #8
Betsy Ross

Great Black Heroes:
    Five Brave Explorers
Fossils Tell of Long Ago
If You Lived in Colonial Times
Rain Forest
It's Mine
Tortillitas para Máma
Justin and the Best Biscuits
    in the World
A River Ran Wild
Llama Pajamas
Finding the Titanic
The Magic School Bus
    Inside the Earth
Have You Seen Bugs?
Wanted Dead or Alive: The True
    Story of Harriet Tubman
Uncle Jed's Barbershop
Wild Weather: Hurricanes!
Tiger Math

Level Q

Class Clown
If You Traveled West in a
    Covered Wagon
Day of the Blizzard
Homer Price
Encyclopedia Brown
    Takes the Cake!
Charlotte's Web
The Hundred Penny Box
Dear Mr. Henshaw
I Have a Dream: The Story
    of Martin Luther King
Thomas Alva Edison
Nothing's Fair in the Fifth Grade
Little House on the Prairie

Sarah Morton's Day
The Velveteen Rabbit
There's a Hamster in My Lunchbox
Bunnicula
True Stories About Abraham
Lincoln
James and the Giant Peach
The True Story of the 3 Little Pigs
Superfudge

Level R

The Adventures of Spider
And Then What Happened,
    Paul Revere?
Gentle Annie
Charlie and the Chocolate Factory
The Great Kapok Tree
Where Was Patrick Henry
    on the 29th of May?
Kid Power
Harry Houdini
Martin Luther King Day
Sadako and the Thousand
    Paper Cranes
Pirates Don't Wear Pink Sunglasses
Sarah, Plain and Tall
The Secret Soldier
Shiloh
Snow Treasure
Stuart Little
Teacher's Pet
The Cricket in Times Square
Weather Words and What
    They Mean
The Enormous Egg

Level S

Catwings
Eureka! It's an Airplane
If You Grew Up with
    George Washington
50 Simple Things Kids Can Do
    to Save the Earth
Lon Po Po
The Cybil War
Misty of Chincoteague
Selena
Phoebe the Spy
Facts and Fun about the Presidents
A Picture Book of Harriet Tubman
Sideways Arithmetic from
    Wayside School
The Rough-Faced Girl
Standing Tall: The Stories of
    Ten Hispanic Americans
Samuel's Choice
Young Merlin Trilogy
The Story of the White House
Fifth Grade: Here Comes Trouble
Sweet Clara and the Freedom Quilt
From the Mixed-Up Files of
    Mrs. Basil E. Frankweiler

Level T

Animorphs #4: The Message
The Book of Spine Tinglers:
Tales to Make You Shiver
Fur, Feathers, and Flippers
Discovering Jupiter:
    The Amazing Collision in Space
Losing Joe's Place
The Watsons Go to
    Birmingham—1963

Mr. Popper's Penguins
Tracker
Mufaro's Beautiful Daughters
Trout Summer
Navajo Long Walk
A Ballad of the Civil War
SOS Titanic
Frederick Douglass
    Fights for Freedom
Steal Away
Harry Potter and the
    Sorcerer's Stone
They Came from Centerfield
Shh! We're Writing
    the Constitution
Zlata's Diary: A Child's
    Life in Sarajevo
The Lion, the Witch and
    the Wardrobe

Level U

The Story of Harriet Tubman:
    Freedom Train
Do the Funky Pickle
My Side of the Mountain
The Girl with the Silver Eyes
P.S. Longer Letter Later
The Jungle Book
Remember the Ladies
The Wright Brothers
Report to the Principal's Office
This Teacher Is Tops!
Rosa Parks
Kids & Co.
Tangerine
Help Is On the Way
The Fledgling
Woodsong
Benjamin Franklin

Level V

A Pocket Full of Seeds
Little Rock Nine
Anne of Green Gables
So Scary!
Dogsong
Hoax!
Foster's War
Spare the Mare!
Sojourner Truth
Maniac Magee
The Golden Goblet
Rascal
The Life and Words of
    Martin Luther King, Jr.
The Secret of Nimh
Stealing Home: The Story
    of Jackie Robinson
The Twenty-One Balloons
The Kids' Guide to Money
Michelle Kwan: My Story
Titanic
Dustland

Level W

Dragon's Gate
Moccasin Trail
The Star Fisher
A Solitary Blue
Torn Thread
Black Eagles: African Americans
    in Aviation
Local News
Mama, Let's Dance
Edwin Hubble:
    American Astronomer
Saving the Animals

Level X

Harriet Beecher Stowe
    and the Beecher's Preachers
The Iceberg Hermit
Quilt Trilogy: #3 The Blue Door
Not Guilty
The Dark Is Rising
The Glory Field
The Forgotten Hiding Place
Nelson Mandela: No Easy
    Walk to Freedom
Katarina
The Rain Ghost
Definitely Cool
Gulf

Level Y

Jackaroo
Jesse
The Call of the Wild
Toning the Sweep
Stories of the North
White Fang
New Kids in Town
Arthur Ashe: Of Tennis
    & the Human Spirit

Level Z

Scorpions
The Adventures of
    Huckleberry Finn
Beyond Belief
Clockwork
Invincible Louisa
Baby-Snatcher
From the Notebooks of
    Melanin Sun

TECHNOLOGY

In each level, carefully chosen web sites have been included. Some of these web sites are for the students. Use them for independent and group extension activities. Most provide additional information great for learning more about the book's topic, author, or genre.

In addition, teacher web sites are provided. These offer additional information about the books and their authors, as well as links to other sites containing lesson materials and resources. One great site that is always available is **www.scholastic.com**, which provides teacher, student, and parent resources for a wealth of books.

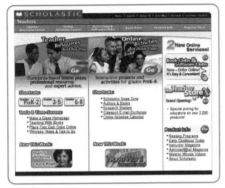

teacher resources

student activities

Reading Counts! quizzes are available for all the titles in the Guided Reading Program. These quizzes can be used to monitor student comprehension and make decisions about each student's instructional needs.

Dear Family Member:

Your child is becoming a skilled independent reader! And the guided reading books that your reader will bring home are designed to help in this process.

As part of *The Scholastic Guided Reading Program*, your child will participate in small groups and will receive individualized instruction to develop fluency, oral language, vocabulary, phonics, comprehension, and writing skills. In addition, your child will bring home enjoyable, level-appropriate stories and selections that will help him or her ensure success as an independent reader.

Here are some suggestions for helping your child before, during, and after reading:

Before

- **Look at the book cover with your child. Together, review the illustrations or photographs in the book. Ask your child to predict what the story or selection will be about.**
- **Discuss what you and your child might already know about the topic of the book you are about to read.**
- **If your child is a beginning reader, echo-read the story or selection with your child by reading a line first and having your child read it after you. If your child is a more skilled reader, periodically stop and ask questions.**

During

- **If your child does not recognize a word right away, help him or her to focus on the familiar letters and spelling patterns in the word. Guide your child to think about other words that look like the unfamiliar word.**
- **Encourage your child to use phonics and decoding skills to sound out any new, unfamiliar words. If necessary, provide the word if your child struggles.**
- **Encourage your child to read with expression and to enjoy reading!**

After

- **Encourage your child to reread the story or selection to develop confidence. If the book is long, reread a few favorite sections or chapters. Perhaps your child could read the story or selection to other family members or friends.**
- **Discuss the story or selection with your child. Ask questions such as: What were your favorite parts? Who were your favorite characters? Why? What interesting fact did you learn?**
- **Have your child keep a journal of favorite stories and selections and interesting words in those books. Your child might also like to write about the book in this journal.**

Have fun with this reading experience and your child will be sure to have fun, too!

Sincerely,

Estimado padre o tutor:

Su niño o niña se está convirtiendo en un lector hábil e independiente. Los libros de lectura guiada que su niño o niña traerá a casa han sido concebidos para ayudarlo(a) a seguir desarrollando sus destrezas de lectura.

Como parte *del Programa de Lectura Guiada de Scholastic*, su niño o niña recibirá instrucción en grupos pequeños e individualizada con el objetivo de desarrollar la fluidez, el lenguaje oral, el vocabulario, la fonética, la comprensión y las destrezas de escritura. Además, su niño o niña traerá a casa cuentos y lecturas amenos y apropiados a su nivel, los cuales le servirán para garantizar su éxito como lector independiente.

Éstas son algunas sugerencias para ayudar a su niño o niña antes, durante y después de la lectura:

Antes

- Observe con su niño o niña la cubierta del libro. Repasen juntos las ilustraciones o fotografías del libro. Pídale a su niño o niña que prediga de qué tratará el cuento o la selección que van a leer.
- Comenten lo que usted y su niño o niña ya sepan sobre el tema del libro que van a leer.
- Si su niño o niña es un lector principiante, lea usted primero una línea y pídale a su niño o niña que lea esa misma línea después. Si su niño o niña es un lector más avanzado, haga una pausa de vez en cuando para hacerle preguntas.

Durante

- Si a su niño o niña le resulta difícil reconocer alguna palabra, ayúdelo(a) a fijarse en las letras y patrones ortográficos de la palabra con los que esté familiarizado. Guíe a su niño o niña en la búsqueda de otras palabras que se parezcan a la palabra desconocida.
- Anime a su niño o niña a usar la fonética y las destrezas de decodificación para leer en voz alta cualquier palabra nueva o desconocida. Si su niño o niña tiene dificultades para hacerlo de manera independiente, dígale la palabra.
- Anime a su niño a leer de manera expresiva y a disfrutar la lectura.

Después

- Anime a su niño o niña a volver a leer el cuento o la selección para que gane en confianza como lector. Si el libro es demasiado largo, vuelva a leer algunas de las secciones o pasajes favoritos de su niño o niña. Otra posibilidad es que su niño o niña les lea el cuento a otros familiares o amigos.
- Comente con su niño o niña el cuento o la selección. Hágale preguntas como las siguientes: ¿Qué partes te gustaron más? ¿Qué personajes son tus favoritos? ¿Por qué? ¿Qué hecho o dato importante aprendiste leyendo este libro?
- Pídale a su niño o niña que lleve un diario de sus cuentos y selecciones favoritos, así como de las palabras interesantes que encuentre en los mismos. También, puede agregar al diario comentarios sobre el libro.

Pase un buen rato leyendo. ¡Su niño o niña, de seguro, también lo disfrutará!

Atentamente,

Guided Reading Skills & Strategies Chart

Level	Title	Genre	Comprehension Strategies	Phonics and Word-Solving Strategies	Writing Options	Technology	Web Site Sponsor
A	Big and Little	Science Nonfiction	Understanding Concepts	Listening For Syllables / Recognizing Phonogram -ig	Descriptive	www.math.com/teachers.html	Math.com
	Games	Social Studies Nonfiction	Recognizing Patterned Text	Using Context / Using Beginning Sounds	Descriptive / Expository	www.gameskidsplay.net	Games Kids Play
	I Can, We Can	Social Studies Nonfiction	Identifying Main Idea	Reading Action Words / Recognizing Pronouns I and We	Expository / Graphic Aid	www.scholastic.com	Scholastic
	In the Woods	Fantasy	Recognizing Story Sequence	Recognizing Rhyming Words / Reading Words With -og	Narrative / Descriptive	www.storiestogrowby.com	Whootie Owl's Stories to Grow By
	Kittens	Concept Book: Counting	Recognizing Punctuation	Reading High-Frequency Words / Reading Numerals	Narrative / Descriptive	www.animaland.org	American Society for the Prevention of Cruelty to Animals
	Let's Go!	Concept Book: Transportation	Understanding Genre: Photo Essay	Reading High-Frequency Words / Understanding Contractions	Descriptive / Expository	education.dot.gov/k5/gamk5.htm	"Transportation Wonderland" from the U.S. Department of Transportation
	My Color	Concept Book: Colors	Using Adjectives	Reading High-Frequency Words / Using Beginning Sounds	Descriptive / Descriptive	www.nwf.org/kids	National Wildlife Federation
	School	Social Studies Nonfiction	Developing Print Awareness	Reading High-Frequency Words / Reading Plurals	Narrative / Expository	www.scholastic.com	Scholastic
	We Can!	Realistic Fiction	Recognizing Setting	Reading High-Frequency Words / Recognizing Phonogram -an	Narrative / Graphic Aid	www.scholastic.com	Scholastic
	What Bears Like	Science Nonfiction	Using Picture Details	Using Context / Using Beginning Sounds	Descriptive / Expository	www.nwf.org/kids	National Wildlife Federation
B	Baby Animals Learn	Science Nonfiction	Comparing/Contrasting	Reading Words With Consonant Blends / Matching Same Sounds	Descriptive / Persuasive	www.sandiegozoo.org	San Diego Zoo
	Carrots	Science Nonfiction	Recognizing Setting	Reading Unfamiliar Words / Matching Same Sounds	Expository / Descriptive	www.kidsgardening.com	National Gardening Association
	Goldilocks	Folktale	Making Predictions	Recognizing Punctuation / Reading Plural Words	Descriptive / Narrative	www.storiestogrowby.com	Whootie Owl's Stories to Grow By
	Hop In!	Fantasy	Distinguishing Fantasy/Reality	Reading Words With Short Vowels / Using Punctuation	Persuasive / Narrative	www.scholastic.com	Scholastic
	Kites	Concept Book: Colors	Using Illustrations	Reading Compound Words / Reading Rhyming Words	Descriptive / Narrative	www.kites.org/zoo	The Virtual Kite Zoo
	Two Can Do It!	Social Studies Nonfiction	Understanding Concepts	Reading Unfamiliar Words / Recognizing Homophones	Descriptive / Descriptive	www.scholastic.com	Scholastic
	Water	Science Nonfiction	Comparing/Contrasting	Using Beginning Sounds / Reading Compound Words	Descriptive / Descriptive	ga.water.usgs.gov/edu	"Water Science for Schools" from the U.S. Geological Survey
	We Are Painting	Concept Book: Counting	Understanding Concepts	Reading Color Words / Reading Plurals	Descriptive / Narrative	www.crayola.com	Crayola
	We Like to Play!	Realistic Fiction	Recognizing Setting	Reading Action Words / Reading High-Frequency Words	Descriptive / Narrative	www.scholastic.com	Scholastic
	What Am I?	Concept Book: Shapes	Recognizing Questions	Understanding Rebuses / Reading High-Frequency Words	Descriptive / Expository	www.math.com/teachers.html	Math.com
C	At Work	Science Nonfiction	Using Illustrations	Reading Words That Look Similar / Reading Plurals	Expository / Descriptive	www.animaland.org	American Society for the Prevention of Cruelty to Animals
	Bugs!	Science Nonfiction	Reading Questions and Answers	Reading Number Words / Reading Compound Words	Descriptive / Persuasive	www.nwf.org/kids	National Wildlife Federation
	Frog Egg to Robin	Science Nonfiction	Understanding Concepts	Reading Plurals / Matching Same Sounds	Descriptive / Expository	www.aviary.org	The National Aviary
	How Many Can Play?	Concept Book	Recognizing Patterned Text	Reading Compound Words / Reading Unfamiliar Words	Descriptive / Expository	www.jumpingforjoy.org/games.html	Jumping For Joy
	I Can Run	Concept Book: Actions	Recognizing Patterned Text	Reading Words With Consonant Blends / Using Punctuation	Narrative / Expository	www.scholastic.com	Scholastic
	I See Fish	Science Nonfiction	Comparing/Contrasting	Reading High-Frequency Words / Recognizing Questions	Descriptive / Persuasive	www.aqua.org	National Aquarium in Baltimore
	It's a Party	Concept Book: Celebrations	Using Photographs	Reading Contractions / Matching Same Sounds	Descriptive / Descriptive	www.kidsparties.com/traditions.htm	"Birthday Traditions From Around the World" from Kids Parties Connection
	Joshua James Likes Trucks	Concept Book	Making Predictions	Matching Same Sounds / Using Context	Descriptive / Descriptive	www.scholastic.com	Scholastic
	Pancakes, Crackers, and Pizza: A Book About Shapes	Concept Book: Shapes	Reading Long Sentences	Reading Food Words / Reading Compound Words	Descriptive / Descriptive	www.math.com/teachers.html	Math.com
	Rain	Concept Book: Colors	Recognizing Story Sequence	Reading Compound Words / Reading Color Words	Narrative / Descriptive	ga.water.usgs.gov/edu	"Water Science for Schools" from the U.S. Geological Survey

Level	Title	Genre	Comprehension Strategies	Phonics and Word-Solving Strategies	Writing Options	Technology	Web Site Sponsor
D	Footprints in the Snow	Science Nonfiction	Relating to Personal Experiences	Recognizing Verbs / Using Punctuation	Expository / Descriptive	www.nwf.org/kids	National Wildlife Federation
	I Know Karate	Informational Fiction	Using Illustrations	Recognizing Verbs / Reading High-Frequency Words	Descriptive	www.scholastic.com	Scholastic
	Nests, Nests, Nests	Science Nonfiction	Comparing/Contrasting	Reading Words With Consonant Blends / Reading Plurals	Descriptive / Descriptive	www.aviary.org	The National Aviary
	One Happy Classroom	Concept Book: Counting	Recognizing Story Pattern	Working With Word Parts / Reading Compound Words	Descriptive / Descriptive	www.scholastic.com	Scholastic
	Paul the Pitcher	Realistic Fiction	Understanding Concepts	Reading Words With Short i / Reading Words That Are Opposites	Descriptive / Descriptive	www.kidsdomain.com/sports/baseball	"Baseball Fun" from Kids Domain
	Rain! Rain!	Informational Fiction	Recognizing Story Sequence	Reading Rhyming Words / Reading High-Frequency Words	Narrative / Descriptive	ga.water.usgs.gov/edu	"Water Science for Schools" from the U.S. Geological Survey
	Ten Cats Have Hats	Concept Book: Counting	Recognizing Sentence Pattern	Reading Rhyming Words / Reading Number Words	Narrative / Narrative	www.math.com/teachers.html	Math.com
	Too Many Balloons	Concept Book: Colors	Reading Environmental Print	Matching Same Sounds / Reading Plurals	Descriptive / Descriptive	www.crayola.com	Crayola
	Where Do Birds Live?	Science Nonfiction	Understanding Concepts	Using Beginning Sounds / Listening for Vowel Sounds	Expository / Expository	www.sandiegozoo.org	San Diego Zoo
	Who Am I?	Concept Book: Jobs	Using Illustrations	Reading Words With -er / Reading Compound Words	Descriptive / Descriptive	www.bls.gov/k12/html/edu_over.htm	The Bureau of Labor Statistics' Career Information
E	Animal Babies	Science Nonfiction	Recognizing Patterned Text	Reading Contractions / Reading Words With Long e	Expository / Poetry	www.animaland.org	American Society for the Prevention of Cruelty to Animals
	A Box Can Be Many Things	Realistic Fiction	Reading Everyday Speech	Reading Unfamiliar Words / Reading Words With /ou/	Descriptive / Poetry	www.scholastic.com	Scholastic
	A Buzz Is Part of a Bee	Concept Book	Using Illustrations	Reading Rhyming Words / Reading Words With Consonant Digraphs	Graphic Aid / Expository	gears.tucson.ars.ag.gov	Carl Hayden Bee Research Center
	Clay Art with Gloria Elliott	Nonfiction	Understanding Setting	Reading Words With Long a / Reading Plurals	Descriptive / Expository	www.handsoncrafts.org	Hands on Crafts
	I Can See	Concept Book: Letters	Comparing/Contrasting	Reading Words With Short a / Matching Same Sounds	Descriptive / Descriptive	www.scholastic.com	Scholastic
	Just Like Me	Realistic Fiction	Using Illustrations	Using Common Spelling Patterns / Matching Same Sounds	Descriptive / Descriptive	www.grolier.com	Grolier
	Look! I Can Read!	Realistic Fiction	Recognizing Questions	Reading Compound Words / Recognizing Rhyming Words	Descriptive / Persuasive	www.readroom.com	The Reading Room
	Polar Babies	Science Nonfiction	Understanding Character	Using Punctuation / Reading Words With Short i	Descriptive / Narrative	www.nwf.org/kids	National Wildlife Federation
	Up, Up, and Away: The Story of Amelia Earhart	Biography	Understanding Character	Reading Words With -ed / Reading Words With Consonant Blends	Expository / Expository	www.nationalaviation.org	National Aviation Hall of Fame
	The Voyage of Mae Jemison	Biography	Recognizing Story Sequence	Reading Words With -ing / Reading Words That Look Similar	Descriptive / Expository	www.nasa.gov/kids.html	NASA "Just For Kids"
F	Amy Loves the Snow	Realistic Fiction	Recognizing Setting	Reading Compound Words / Recognizing Contractions and Possessives	Expository / Narrative	www.wildwildweather.com	Dan's Wild Wild Weather Page
	Cookie's Week	Concept Book: Days of the Week	Understanding Cause/Effect	Reading Compound Words / Reading Words With r-Controlled Vowels	Expository / Narrative	www.animaland.org	American Society for the Prevention of Cruelty to Animals
	Firehouse Sal	Informational Fiction	Making Predictions	Reading Number Words / Reading Words With Consonant Blends	Expository / Graphic Aid	www.nfpa.org/sparky	"Sparky the Fire Dog" web site from The National Fire Protection Association
	Frog's Lunch	Informational Fiction	Reading Dialogue	Reading Words With -ing and -ed / Reading Words With Consonant Blends	Expository / Narrative	www.exploratorium.edu/frogs	The Exploratorium's Frogs Exhibition
	Harry's House	Informational Fiction	Drawing Conclusions	Distinguishing Between Nouns and Verbs / Recognizing Contractions and Possessives	Expository / Expository	www.animaland.org	American Society for the Prevention of Cruelty to Animals
	I Am Fire	Science Nonfiction	Relating to Personal Experiences	Reading Words With Long i / Reading Unfamiliar Words	Expository / Expository	www.nfpa.org/sparky	"Sparky the Fire Dog" web site from The National Fire Protection Association
	Is This You?	Concept Book: How-to	Using Illustrations	Reading High-Frequency Words / Reading Words With Long a and Long e	Expository / Expository	www.scholastic.com	Scholastic
	Pizza Party!	Realistic Fiction	Understanding Story Development	Reading Rhyming Words / Reading Action Words	Expository / Narrative	www.kidfood.org	Kid Food CyberClub
	Shine, Sun!	Informational Fiction	Recognizing Setting	Reading Words With Digraphs / Reading High-Frequency Words	Expository / Graphic Aid	www.americansun.org	American Sun Protection Association
	Soccer Game!	Realistic Fiction	Making Inferences	Reading Rhyming Words / Reading Verbs	Narrative / Narrative	www.soccerjr.com	Soccer Jr. Magazine

Level	Title	Genre	Comprehension Strategies	Phonics and Word-Solving Strategies	Writing Options	Technology	Web Site Sponsor
G	The Class Trip	Realistic Fiction	Relating to Personal Experiences	Reading Verbs; Reading Words With Consonant Blends	Descriptive; Expository	www.sandiegozoo.org	San Diego Zoo
	Dinosaurs	Science Nonfiction	Comparing/Contrasting	Using Context; Using Picture Details	Descriptive; Graphic Aid	www.amnh.org	American Museum of Natural History
	The Great Race	Fantasy	Reading Dialogue	Reading Words With oo; Reading Sound Words	Expository; Narrative	www.scholastic.com	Scholastic
	Make It Move!	Science Nonfiction	Recognizing Questions	Reading Pronouns; Blending Words	Descriptive; Graphic Aid	www.mos.org	Boston Museum of Science
	Pele: The King of Soccer	Biography	Making Inferences	Reading Words With -ed; Reading Words With Short i	Graphic Aid; Descriptive	www.soccerjr.com	Soccer Jr. Magazine
	Sam the Garbage Hound	Realistic Fiction	Comparing/Contrasting	Reading Words With g; Reading Adjectives	Narrative; Graphic Aid	www.animaland.org	American Society for the Prevention of Cruelty to Animals
	Sometimes Things Change	Science Nonfiction	Making Predictions	Reading Words With Consonant Blends; Reading High-Frequency Words	Descriptive; Expository	ga.water.usgs.gov/edu	"Water Science for Schools" from the U.S. Geological Survey
	Teddy Bear for Sale	Fantasy	Making Inferences	Reading Directional Words; Recognizing Verbs	Narrative; Descriptive	www.theodoreroosevelt.org	Theodore Roosevelt Association
	Wait, Skates!	Realistic Fiction	Recognizing Story Sequence	Reading Words With Long a; Reading Punctuation	Narrative; Narrative	www.grolier.com	Grolier
	Why Can't I Fly?	Fantasy	Recognizing Plot	Reading Words With Long i; Reading Rhyming Words	Poetry; Narrative	www.animalsoftherainforest.com	The Jason Project
H	Caps, Hats, Socks, and Mittens: A Book About the Four Seasons	Concept Book: Seasons	Making Inferences	Reading Words With s-Blends; Understanding Figurative Language	Descriptive; Narrative	kids.earth.nasa.gov	"For Kids Only - Earth Science Enterprise" from NASA
	Come! Sit! Speak!	Realistic Fiction	Recognizing Setting	Reading Words With Long o; Reading Difficult Words	Descriptive; Graphic Aid	www.howtoloveyourdog.com	How to Love Your Dog: A Kid's Guide to Dog Care
	Danny and the Dinosaur Go to Camp	Fantasy	Distinguishing Fantasy/Reality	Reading Words With Long o; Reading Unfamiliar Words	Narrative; Descriptive	www.amnh.org	American Museum of Natural History
	It's Spring!	Informational Fiction	Summarizing	Reading Words With Long i	Poetry; Narrative	www.favoritepoem.org	The Favorite Poem Project
	A Kiss for Little Bear	Fantasy	Understanding Character	Reading Words With ow; Recognizing Synonyms	Graphic Aid; Persuasive	www.scholastic.com	Scholastic
	My Pigs	Nonfiction	Recognizing Main Idea	Reading Words With Long e; Reading Pronouns	Graphic Aid; Expository	www.animaland.org	American Society for the Prevention of Cruelty to Animals
	Plane Rides	Nonfiction	Understanding Story Sequence	Reading Words With Long i; Reading Plural Words	Expository; Descriptive	www.nasm.si.edu	National Air and Space Museum
	The Very Big Potato	Folktale	Recognizing Cause/Effect	Reading Words With Long i and Long a; Reading Compound Words	Persuasive; Narrative	www.kidsgardening.com	National Gardening Association
	What Will the Weather Be Like Today?	Science Nonfiction	Understanding Cause/Effect	Reading Contractions; Reading Words With Long i	Expository; Descriptive	www.wildwildweather.com	Dan's Wild Wild Weather Page
	When I First Came to This Land	Historical Fiction	Understanding Poetic Language	Reading Words With r-Blends; Reading Multisyllabic Words; Using Common Spelling Patterns; Reading Words With r-Controlled Vowels	Persuasive; Descriptive	www.favoritepoem.org	The Favorite Poem Project
I	All Tutus Should Be Pink	Realistic Fiction	Understanding Theme	Reading Words With Long e; Understanding Plurals	Expository; Narrative	www.abt.org	American Ballet Theatre
	A Day with a Mail Carrier	Social Studies Nonfiction	Summarizing	Reading Words With Long a; Reading Unfamiliar Words	Expository; Persuasive	www.si.edu/postal	National Postal Museum
	A Day with Firefighters	Social Studies Nonfiction	Making Inferences	Reading Words With Long o; Using Common Spelling Patterns	Expository; Descriptive	www.nfpa.org/sparky	"Sparky the Fire Dog" web site from The National Fire Protection Association
	The Elves and the Shoemaker	Fairy Tale	Understanding Plot	Reading Words With -ed; Reading Contractions and Possessives	Expository; Narrative	www.storiestogrowby.com	Whootie Owl's Stories to Grow By
	Goldilocks and the Three Bears	Fairy Tale	Understanding Cause/Effect	Recognizing Synonyms; Reading Homophones	Expository; Narrative	www.storiestogrowby.com	Whootie Owl's Stories to Grow By
	I Am a Rock	Science Nonfiction	Reading for Information	Reading Multisyllabic Words; Reading Words With -er	Graphic Aid; Descriptive	www.usgs.gov/education	U.S. Geological Survey
	Messy Bessey's Family Reunion	Realistic Fiction	Recognizing Setting	Reading Words That Rhyme; Reading Compound Words	Expository; Narrative	www.scholastic.com	Scholastic
	Red-Eyed Tree Frog	Science Nonfiction	Reading for Information	Reading Words With Long e; Reading Words With Blends	Narrative; Expository	www.animalsoftherainforest.com	The Jason Project
	The Sun's Family of Planets	Science Nonfiction	Understanding Concepts	Reading Unfamiliar Words; Reading Words With -est	Graphic Aid; Narrative	www.nasa.gov/kids.html	NASA "Just For Kids"
	We Just Moved!	Fiction	Relating to Personal Experiences	Reading Compound Words; Reading Words With r-Controlled Vowels	Narrative; Descriptive	www.castles.org	Castles of the World

Level	Title	Genre	Comprehension Strategies	Phonics and Word-Solving Strategies	Writing Options	Technology	Web Site Sponsor
J	Bear Shadow	Fantasy	Identifying Problems/Solutions	Recognizing Base Words; Recognizing Irregular Past-Tense Verbs	Narrative, Persuasive	www.exploratorium.edu	The Exploratorium
	Henry and Mudge and the Long Weekend	Realistic Fiction	Understanding Character	Recognizing Base Words; Understanding Similes	Narrative, Expository	www.howtoloveyourdog.com	How to Love Your Dog: A Kid's Guide to Dog Care
	How Kittens Grow	Science Nonfiction	Understanding Cause/Effect	Reading Words With Long a; Reading Words With Suffixes	Expository, Poetry	www.animaland.org	American Society for the Prevention of Cruelty to Animals
	Jack Plays the Violin	Realistic Fiction	Making Predictions	Reading Words With Consonant Blends; Understanding Multiple Meaning Words	Graphic Aid, Narrative	www.playmusic.org	American Symphony Orchestra League
	Looking at Maps and Globes	Social Studies Nonfiction	Using Maps and Globes	Reading Words With Consonant /j/g; Understanding Common and Proper Nouns	Graphic Aid, Descriptive	www.nationalgeographic.com/maps	National Geographic Maps and Geography
	Me on the Map	Social Studies Nonfiction	Using Maps and Charts	Understanding Common and Proper Nouns; Reading Words With s-Blends	Graphic Aid, Expository	www.mapquest.com	MapQuest
	My Life	Autobiography	Comparing/Contrasting	Reading Multisyllabic Words; Understanding Plurals	Expository, Narrative	www.scholastic.com	Scholastic
	On the Lake	Informational Fiction	Making Inferences	Using Context; Recognizing Homophones	Expository, Descriptive	www.boatsafe.com/kids	International Marine Educators, Inc.
	Poppleton Everyday	Fantasy	Understanding Sequence	Reading Compound Words	Narrative, Descriptive	www.scholastic.com	Scholastic
	The Sword in the Stone	Legend	Understanding Plot	Recognizing Contractions and Possessives; Reading Words With Silent Letters; Reading Words With Long i	Narrative, Expository	www.2020site.org/kingarthur	"King Arthur's Legends" from 2020site.org
K	All About Things People Do	Social Studies Nonfiction	Reading for Information	Reading Words With Suffixes; Reading Multisyllabic Words	Expository, Descriptive	www.bls.gov/k12/html/edu_over.htm	The Bureau of Labor Statistics' Career Information
	The Blue Mittens	Realistic Fiction	Comparing/Contrasting	Reading Words With Final e; Recognizing Homophones	Descriptive, Poetry	www.scholastic.com	Scholastic
	Chickens Aren't the Only Ones	Science Nonfiction	Comparing/Contrasting	Recognizing Contractions and Possessives; Reading Multisyllabic Words	Descriptive, Graphic Aid	www.enature.com	Enature
	The Day Jimmy's Boa Ate the Wash	Fantasy	Understanding Cause/Effect	Reading Informal Speech; Reading Words With -ed, -ing	Expository, Graphic Aid	www.animaland.org	American Society for the Prevention of Cruelty to Animals
	Ming Lo Moves the Mountain	Folktale	Understanding Character	Recognizing Base Words	Graphic Aid, Poetry	www.storiestogrowby.com	Whootie Owl's Stories to Grow By
	Our Flag	Social Studies Nonfiction	Understanding Cause/Effect	Understanding Irregular Past-Tense Verbs; Recognizing Synonyms	Descriptive, Descriptive	americanhistory.si.edu	National Museum of American History
	Penguins	Science Nonfiction	Recognizing Setting	Reading Words With Suffixes; Understanding Plurals	Expository, Graphic Aid	www.nwf.org/kids	National Wildlife Federation
	A Place for Grace	Informational Fiction	Identifying Problems/Solutions	Reading Words With -ed; Reading Words With -ly	Expository, Graphic Aid	www.handspeak.com	HandSpeak: A Sign Language Dictionary Online
	Shipwreck Saturday	Realistic Fiction	Understanding Point of View	Reading Words With Final e; Understanding Figurative Language	Narrative, Narrative	www.enchantedlearning.com/crafts/origami	"Origami KinderCrafts" from EnchantedLearning.com
	What Magnets Can Do	Science Nonfiction	Reading for Information	Reading Compound Words; Reading Variations of Words	Descriptive, Descriptive	www.exploratorium.edu	The Exploratorium
L	Animal Tracks	Science Nonfiction	Categorizing Information	Reading Possessives; Reading Words With -ing	Narrative, Expository	www.nwf.org/kids	National Wildlife Federation
	Apatosaurus	Science Nonfiction	Reading for Information	Reading Unfamiliar Words; Understanding Suffixes	Expository, Expository	www.amnh.org	American Museum of Natural History
	The Big "M"	Informational Fiction	Making Predictions	Reading Difficult Words; Reading Words With -ed	Narrative, Persuasive	www.metmuseum.org	The Metropolitan Museum of Art
	Cam Jansen and the Mystery of the Babe Ruth Baseball	Mystery	Understanding Character	Using Context; Reading Number Words	Graphic Aid, Narrative	kids.mysterynet.com	MysteryNet's Kids Mysteries
	The Mud Pony	Folktale	Making Predictions	Reading Contractions; Reading Compound Words	Narrative, Narrative	www.nmai.si.edu	National Museum of the American Indian
	Play Ball, Amelia Bedelia	Fiction	Comparing/Contrasting	Understanding Idiomatic Expressions; Reading Dialogue	Persuasive, Narrative	www.kidsdomain.com/sports/baseball	"Baseball Fun" from Kids Domain
	Rain Forest	Science Nonfiction	Using Maps and Diagrams	Reading Multisyllabic Words; Reading Words With r-Controlled Vowels	Persuasive, Expository	www.ran.org	Rainforest Action Network
	Solve It!	Mystery	Making Inferences	Reading Informal Speech; Understanding Homophones	Persuasive, Persuasive	kids.mysterynet.com	MysteryNet's Kids Mysteries
	Spiders	Science Nonfiction	Categorizing Information	Reading Plurals and Possessives; Reading Multisyllabic Words	Expository, Poetry	www.enature.com	Enature
	This Is My House	Social Studies Nonfiction	Comparing/Contrasting	Understanding Plurals; Reading Difficult Words	Descriptive, Descriptive	www.whyy.org/aie	The Foundation For Architecture's Architecture in Education Program

Level	Title	Genre	Comprehension Strategies	Phonics and Word-Solving Strategies	Writing Options	Technology	Web Site Sponsor
M	At 1600 Pennsylvania Avenue	Social Studies Nonfiction	Categorizing Information	Reading Words With r-Controlled Vowels / Recognizing Proper Nouns and Titles	Graphic Aid / Expository	www.whitehouse.gov	The White House
	Boom!	Science Nonfiction	Using Diagrams	Reading Words With /oo/ / Identifying Open and Closed Syllables	Poetry / Graphic Aid	www.usgs.gov	U.S. Geological Survey
	Buddy: The First Seeing Eye Dog	Nonfiction	Understanding Chapters	Reading Words With -ed / Recognizing Contractions	Descriptive / Narrative	www.nfb.org	National Federation of the Blind
	California or Bust!	Historical Fiction	Understanding Setting	Reading Words With Prefixes / Using Context	Expository / Expository	www.americaslibrary.gov	"America's Story" from the Library of Congress
	Firefighters	Social Studies Nonfiction	Recognizing Main Idea/Details	Identifying Open Syllables / Reading Words With Final e	Expository / Descriptive	www.nfpa.org/sparky	"Sparky the Fire Dog" web site from The National Fire Protection Association
	Gung Hay Fat Choy	Social Studies Nonfiction	Reading for Information	Recognizing Variations of Words / Recognizing Homophones	Descriptive / Descriptive	www.camla.org	The Chinese American Museum
	Jungle Jack Hanna's Safari Adventure	Nonfiction	Summarizing	Reading Compound Words / Recognizing Strong Verbs	Expository / Expository	www.nwf.org/kids	National Wildlife Federation
	The Littles Go Exploring	Fantasy	Understanding Character	Reading Words With -ly / Reading Informal Speech	Graphic Aid / Descriptive	www.scholastic.com	Scholastic
	Nine True Dolphin Stories	Science Nonfiction	Relating to Personal Experience	Reading Compound Words / Recognizing Specialized Vocabulary	Expository / Graphic Aid	www.wcs.org	Wildlife Conservation Society
	Yellowstone National Park	Social Studies Nonfiction	Understanding Informational Texts	Recognizing Variations of Words / Recognizing Plurals	Graphic Aid / Descriptive	www.nps.gov/yell	Yellowstone National Park
N	Amber Brown Is Feeling Blue	Realistic Fiction	Understanding Character / Understanding Point of View	Reading Words With -y, -ly	Expository / Persuasive	www.scholastic.com	Scholastic
	Catwings Return	Fantasy	Making Inferences / Understanding Sequence	Reading Compound Words	Expository / Descriptive	www.scholastic.com	Scholastic
	The Corn Husk Doll	Informational Fiction	Reading for Information / Using Diagrams	Reading Contractions	Expository / Graphic Aid	www.nmai.si.edu	National Museum of the American Indian
	A Dinosaur Named Sue: The Find of the Century	Science Nonfiction	Summarizing / Recognizing Setting	Reading Words With -ed	Expository / Graphic Aid	www.fieldmuseum.org	The Field Museum of Natural History
	Do Tornadoes Really Twist? Questions and Answers About Tornadoes and Hurricanes	Science Nonfiction	Categorizing Information / Comparing/Contrasting	Reading Words With s-Blends	Descriptive / Expository	www.noaa.gov	National Oceanic and Atmospheric Administration
	Endangered Animals	Science Nonfiction	Recognizing Cause/Effect / Understanding Chapters	Reading Difficult Words	Expository / Persuasive	www.wcs.org	Wildlife Conservation Society
	The Garden on Green Street	Realistic Fiction	Understanding Plot / Understanding Sequence	Reading Words With -ing	Graphic Aid / Persuasive	www.kidsgardening.com	National Gardening Association
	How Is a Crayon Made?	Nonfiction	Understanding Concepts / Relating to Personal Experience	Reading Words With Prefixes	Descriptive / Graphic Aid	www.crayola.com	Crayola
	Lily and Miss Liberty	Historical Fiction	Identifying Problems/Solutions / Understanding Historical Context	Understanding Plurals	Descriptive / Descriptive	www.nps.gov/stli	Statue of Liberty National Monument
	Louis Braille: The Boy Who Invented Books for the Blind	Biography	Understanding Point of View / Story Development	Reading Words With /f/gh/	Descriptive / Expository	www.nfb.org	National Federation of the Blind
O	The Animal Shelter Mystery	Mystery	Understanding Story Development / Making Predictions	Reading Words With Long a and Long e	Persuasive / Narrative	www.scholastic.com	Scholastic
	Desert Life	Science Nonfiction	Summarizing / Recognizing Setting	Reading Words With Diphthong oi, oy	Expository / Descriptive	www.nps.gov/sagu	Saguaro National Park
	Donner Party: A Diary of a Survivor	Social Studies Nonfiction	Reading for Information / Using Diagrams	Reading Contractions	Narrative / Descriptive	www.historyplace.com	The History Place
	Flossie & the Fox	Fantasy	Understanding Plot / Understanding Genre: Fantasy	Using Context	Narrative / Narrative	www.storiestogrowby.com	Whootie Owl's Stories to Grow By
	I Wonder Why Snakes Shed Their Skins and Other Questions About Reptiles	Science Nonfiction	Categorizing Information / Recognizing Cause/Effect	Reading Suffixes	Expository / Descriptive	www.enature.com	Enature
	The Kids' Invention Book	Nonfiction	Understanding Concepts / Relating to Personal Experiences	Reading Multisyllabic Words	Graphic Aid / Narrative	www.sln.org	The Science Learning Network
	Look What Came From Mexico	Social Studies Nonfiction	Understanding Chapters / Comparing/Contrasting	Reading Suffixes	Expository / Descriptive	www.mexonline.com/culture.htm	Mexico Art and Culture Directory
	Miss Rumphius	Fiction	Making Inferences / Understanding Character	Reading Difficult Words	Descriptive / Graphic Aid	www.kidsgardening.com	National Gardening Association

Level	Title	Genre	Comprehension Strategies	Phonics and Word-Solving Strategies	Writing Options	Technology	Web Site Sponsor
O	A Picture Book of Sojourner Truth	Biography	Using Historical Context; Understanding Genre: Biography	Recognizing Colloquialisms	Expository; Expository	www.americaslibrary.gov	"America's Story" from the Library of Congress
	Where There Was Smoke	Social Studies Nonfiction	Identifying Problems/Solutions; Making Predictions	Using Context	Persuasive; Expository	www.nps.gov	National Park Service
P	26 Fairmount Avenue	Autobiography	Relating to Personal Experiences; Understanding Chapters	Reading Multisyllabic Words	Narrative; Descriptive	www.owl.english.perdue.edu	The Purdue University Online Writing Lab
	The Drum Beats On	Social Studies Nonfiction	Understanding Theme; Making Inferences	Reading Words With -ing	Descriptive; Expository	www.nmai.si.edu	National Museum of the American Indian
	The Eagle Has Landed	Social Studies Nonfiction	Understanding Sequence; Understanding Historical Context	Reading Words With Suffixes	Graphic Aid; Persuasive	www.nasm.edu	National Air and Space Museum
	Encyclopedia Brown Carries On	Mystery	Understanding Genre: Mystery; Summarizing	Reading Unfamiliar Words	Narrative; Descriptive	kids.mysterynet.com	MysteryNet's Kids Mysteries
	In the Rain Forest	Science Nonfiction	Recognizing Setting; Understanding Point of View	Reading Unfamiliar Words	Persuasive; Expository	www.ran.org	Rainforest Action Network
	The Magic School Bus Inside a Beehive	Science Nonfiction	Reading for Information; Understanding Plot	Reading Informal Speech	Graphic Aid; Descriptive	www.enature.com	Enature
	The Real McCoy: The Life of an African-American Inventor	Biography	Understanding Historical Context; Understanding Character	Reading Compound Words	Descriptive; Narrative	www.inventorsmuseum.com	Inventors Museum
	Shoebag	Fantasy	Evaluating Author's Purpose; Understanding Story Development	Reading Unfamiliar Words	Persuasive; Descriptive	www.scholastic.com	Scholastic
	Weather	Science Nonfiction	Summarizing; Categorizing Information	Reading Words With Vowel Digraphs	Descriptive; Persuasive	www.wildwildweather.com	Dan's Wild Wild Weather Page
	A Whale Is Not a Fish and Other Animal Mix-ups	Science Nonfiction	Comparing/Contrasting; Understanding Concepts	Understanding Plurals	Expository; Descriptive	www.nwf.org/kids	National Wildlife Federation
Q	Adventures of the Shark Lady: Eugenie Clark Around the World	Biography	Summarizing; Categorizing Information	Understanding Plurals	Graphic Aid; Descriptive	www.aqua.org	National Aquarium in Baltimore
	American Tall Tales	Tall Tale	Understanding Sequence; Understanding Exaggeration	Understanding Figurative Language	Descriptive; Narrative	www.americaslibrary.gov	"America's Story" from the Library of Congress
	Animals of Long Ago	Science Nonfiction	Categorizing Information; Understanding Chapters	Using Context	Graphic Aid; Expository	www.amnh.org	American Museum of Natural History
	Exploring the Titanic	Social Studies Nonfiction	Recognizing Cause/Effect; Comparing/Contrasting	Reading Words With Prefixes	Expository; Narrative	www.encyclopedia-titanica.org	Encyclopedia Titanica
	Favorite Medieval Tales	Legend	Understanding Plot; Understanding Character	Reading Suffixes	Narrative; Expository	www.learner.org/exhibits/middleages	Learner.org
	Folktales from China	Folktale	Making Inferences; Understanding Character	Reading Multisyllabic Words	Narrative; Narrative	www.camla.org	The Chinese American Museum
	Help! I'm Trapped in the First Day of Summer Camp	Fantasy	Understanding Genre: Fantasy; Making Predictions	Recognizing Colloquialisms	Narrative; Narrative	www.scholastic.com	Scholastic
	...If You Lived With the Cherokee	Social Studies Nonfiction	Recognizing Cause/Effect; Summarizing	Reading Unusual Language	Expository; Narrative	www.nmai.si.edu	National Museum of the American Indian
	Mary on Horseback: Three Mountain Stories	Biography	Identifying Problems/Solutions; Recognizing Setting	Reading Dialect	Narrative; Graphic Aid	frontiernursing.org	Frontier Nursing Service
	Native American Art	Social Studies Nonfiction	Making Inferences; Using Captions	Identifying Open Syllables	Descriptive; Expository	www.nmai.si.edu	National Museum of the American Indian
R	And Then What Happened, Paul Revere?	Biography	Reading for Information; Understanding Character	Reading Historical Language	Graphic Aid; Graphic Aid	www.paulreverehouse.org	The Paul Revere House
	Brian's Winter	Realistic Fiction	Recognizing Setting; Making Predictions	Reading Words With Suffixes.	Narrative; Poetry	www.nps.gov	National Park Service
	Draw Me a Story	Biography	Understanding Chapters; Understanding Character	Recognizing Possessives	Expository; Expository	www.scholastic.com	Scholastic
	A Jar of Dreams	Historical Fiction	Understanding Theme; Understanding Point of View	Reading Word Variations	Descriptive; Poetry	americanhistory.si.edu/perfectunion	"A More Perfect Union: Japanese Americans and the U.S. Constitution" from Smithsonian
	Journey to Ellis Island: How My Father Came to America	Social Studies Nonfiction	Understanding Sequence; Understanding Historical Context	Reading Words With Consonant + -le	Persuasive; Expository	www.ellisisland.org	Ellis Island
	The Last Princess: The Story of Princess Ka'iulani of Hawai'i	Biography	Comparing/Contrasting; Understanding Historical Context	Identifying Word Parts	Descriptive; Narrative	www.hawaiianhistory.org	Hawaiian Historical Society
	Lewis and Clark	Social Studies Nonfiction	Making Inferences; Using Primary Sources	Reading Historical Language	Narrative; Graphic Aid	americanhistory.si.edu	National Museum of American History

Level	Title	Genre	Comprehension Strategies	Phonics and Word-Solving Strategies	Writing Options	Technology	Web Site Sponsor
R	Listening to Crickets: A Story about Rachel Carson	Biography	Understanding Chapters / Identifying Problems/Solutions	Reading Words With Suffixes	Graphic Aid / Expository	www.rachelcarson.org	Rachel Carson.org
	Pigs Might Fly	Fantasy	Understanding Point of View / Summarizing	Reading Unusual Language	Descriptive / Narrative	www.scholastic.com	Scholastic
	The Tortoise Shell & Other African Stories	Folktale	Comparing/Contrasting / Understanding Metaphors and Similes	Reading Difficult Words	Narrative / Expository	www.storiestogrowby.com	Whootie Owl's Stories to Grow By
S	Ben and Me	Informational Fiction	Understanding Cause/Effect / Understanding Historical Context	Using Context	Expository / Narrative	www.inventorsmuseum.com	Inventors Museum
	Bessie Coleman	Biography	Understanding Chapters / Understanding Historical Context	Recognizing Variations of Words	Expository / Persuasive	www.firstflight.org	The First Flight Society
	The Broccoli Tapes	Realistic Fiction	Making Predictions / Understanding Character	Distinguishing Homonyms	Narrative / Graphic Aid	www.scholastic.com	Scholastic
	The Chicago Fire	Social Studies Nonfiction	Summarizing / Understanding Sequence	Reading Compound Words	Descriptive / Expository	www.nfpa.org	National Fire Protection Association
	Earthquake! A Story of Old San Francisco	Historical Fiction	Recognizing Setting / Understanding Point of View	Reading Words With Prefixes	Narrative / Graphic Aid	www.historyplace.com	The History Place
	Eureka! It's Television!	Science Nonfiction	Identifying Problems/Solutions / Using Diagrams	Reading Difficult Words	Descriptive / Persuasive	www.mtr.org	The Museum of Television & Radio
	In the Line of Fire: Eight Women War Spies	Biography	Understanding Cause/Effect / Summarizing	Understanding Plurals	Narrative / Expository	www.nwhp.org	National Women's History Project
	In the Year of the Boar and Jackie Robinson	Historical Fiction	Evaluating Author's Purpose / Understanding Theme	Reading Difficult Words	Narrative / Expository	www.baseballhalloffame.org	The National Baseball Hall of Fame
	Salsa Stories	Realistic Fiction	Understanding Point of View / Relating to Personal Experience	Understanding Colloquialisms	Descriptive / Descriptive	www.elmuseo.org	El Museo del Barrio
	The Star Fisher	Historical Fiction	Making Inferences / Understanding Long Sentences	Recognizing Synonyms	Expository / Expository	www.camla.org	The Chinese American Museum
T	The Big Lie: A True Story	Autobiography	Comparing/Contrasting / Understanding Historical Context	Using Context	Narrative / Narrative	www.ushmm.org	U.S. Holocaust Memorial Museum
	The Girl Who Chased Away Sorrow: The Diary of Sarah Nita, a Navajo Girl	Historical Fiction	Making Inferences / Using Maps and Graphic Aids	Reading Words With Consonant + -le	Expository / Persuasive	www.nmai.si.edu	National Museum of the American Indian
	Bonanza Girl	Historical Fiction	Recognizing Setting / Understanding Point of View	Reading Unusual Language	Persuasive / Descriptive	www.pbs.org/goldrush	Public Broadcasting Service
	Sleepers, Wake	Science Fiction	Making Predictions / Understanding Genre: Science Fiction	Reading Multisyllabic Words	Narrative / Persuasive	www.nasa.gov	National Aeronautics and Space Administration (NASA)
	Sounder	Realistic Fiction	Understanding Character / Relating to Personal Experiences	Reading Informal Speech	Narrative / Descriptive	www.americaslibrary.gov	"America's Story" from the Library of Congress
	The Story of Levi's	Biography	Understanding Sequence / Identifying Problems/Solutions	Understanding Compound Words	Narrative / Graphic Aid	www.americaslibrary.gov	"America's Story" from the Library of Congress
	The Tall Tale of John Henry	Tall Tale	Recognizing Cause/Effect / Understanding Theme	Recognizing Colloquialisms	Narrative / Narrative	www.nrhs.com	National Railway Historical Society
	Under the Royal Palms: A Childhood in Cuba	Autobiography	Understanding Genre: Autobiography / Understanding Long Sentences	Recognizing Variations of Words	Expository / Narrative	www.almaada.com	Alma Flor Ada's web site
	Volcano: The Eruption and Healing of Mount St. Helens	Science Nonfiction	Summarizing / Using Diagrams	Reading Words With -ing	Expository / Expository	www.usgs.gov	U.S. Geological Survey
	Where Are the Wolves?	Science Nonfiction	Categorizing Information / Understanding Cause/Effect	Understanding Plurals	Expository / Narrative	www.wolf.org	International Wolf Center
U	First Ladies: Women Who Called the White House Home	Biography	Categorizing Information / Understanding Historical Context	Reading Multisyllabic Words	Expository / Persuasive	www.whitehouse.gov	The White House
	Geysers: When Earth Roars	Science Nonfiction	Reading for Information / Using Diagrams	Reading Words With Suffixes	Expository / Narrative	www.yellowstone.net/geysers	Yellowstone National Park
	Golden Games	Social Studies Nonfiction	Understanding Sequence / Understanding Genre: Nonfiction	Reading Words With Suffixes	Expository / Expository	www.olympic.org	International Olympic Committee
	Great Explorations	Biography	Understanding Main Idea/Details / Categorizing Information	Reading Multisyllabic Words	Expository / Narrative	www.historyplace.com	The History Place
	Hoang Anh: A Vietnamese-American Boy	Biography	Comparing/Contrasting / Summarizing	Understanding Compound Words	Narrative / Graphic Aid	www.pbs.org/kcet/newamericans	*The New Americans* web exhibition from PBS
	An Indian Winter	Social Studies Nonfiction	Understanding Point of View / Using Illustrations	Recognizing Synonyms	Expository / Narrative	www.nmai.si.edu	National Museum of the American Indian

Level	Title	Genre	Comprehension Strategies	Phonics and Word-Solving Strategies	Writing Options	Technology	Web Site Sponsor
U	Midnight Magic	Mystery	Recognizing Setting / Understanding Theme	Using Context Clues	Narrative Descriptive	www.avi-writer.com	Avi's web site
	The Secret Garden	Fiction	Understanding Character / Understanding Plot	Reading Unusual Language	Narrative Narrative	www.scholastic.com	Scholastic
	Sir Arthur	Biography	Making Inferences / Recognizing Cause/Effect	Understanding Plurals	Narrative Expository	www.fbi.gov	Federal Bureau of Investigation
	The Story of My Life	Autobiography	Relating to Personal Experiences / Understanding Figurative Language	Using Context	Descriptive Expository	www.greatwomen.org	National Women's Hall of Fame
V	1000 Facts About Space	Science Nonfiction	Evaluating Author's Purpose / Reading for Information	Reading Multisyllabic Words	Expository Narrative	www.nasa.gov	National Aeronautics and Space Administration (NASA)
	Alice in Wonderland	Fantasy	Understanding Genre: Fantasy / Recognizing Setting	Reading Unusual Language	Descriptive Narrative	www.lewiscarroll.org/carroll.html	Lewis Carroll Society of North America
	Eleanor Roosevelt	Biography	Summarizing / Understanding Historical Context	Reading Words With -ed	Graphic Aid Expository	www.un.org	United Nations
	Get on Board: The Story of the Underground Railroad	Social Studies Nonfiction	Recognizing Setting / Using a Time Line	Reading Words With Suffixes	Expository Narrative	www.undergroundrailroad.org	National Underground Railroad Freedom Center
	Harry Potter and the Chamber of Secrets	Fantasy	Making Predictions / Understanding Theme	Reading Compound Words	Descriptive Descriptive	www.scholastic.com/harrypotter	Scholastic
	How I Came to Be a Writer	Autobiography	Evaluating Author's Purpose / Understanding Genre: Autobiography	Using Common Spelling Patterns	Expository Persuasive	owl.english.purdue.edu	The Purdue University Online Writing Lab
	The Music of Dolphins	Fiction	Making Inferences / Understanding Character	Working With Word Parts	Descriptive Descriptive	www.scholastic.com	Scholastic
	Old Yeller	Realistic Fiction	Making Predictions / Understanding Plot	Recognizing Colloquialisms	Expository Narrative	www.americaslibrary.gov	"America's Story" from the Library of Congress
	The True Confessions of Charlotte Doyle	Historical Fiction	Understanding Point of View / Understanding Diagrams	Using Context	Narrative Narrative	www.historyplace.com	The History Place
	Under Wraps	Social Studies Nonfiction	Recognizing Main Idea/Details / Comparing/Contrasting	Reading Words With Greek or Latin Roots	Expository Expository	www.virtual-egypt.com	Virtual-Egypt.com
W	Buried in Ice: The Mystery of a Lost Arctic Expedition	Social Studies Nonfiction	Identifying Problems/Solutions / Using Graphic Aids	Understanding Denotation and Connotation	Expository Narrative	www.amnh.org	American Museum of Natural History
	Dive! My Adventures in the Deep Frontier	Science Nonfiction	Recognizing Main Idea/Details / Understanding Genre: Science Nonfiction	Identifying Open and Closed Syllables	Expository Expository	www.aqua.org	National Aquarium in Baltimore
	The First Woman Doctor	Biography	Identifying Problems/Solutions / Summarizing	Reading Words With Consonant + -le, -al, -el	Expository Poetry	www.greatwomen.org	National Women's Hall of Fame
	From Rags to Riches	Biography	Understanding Character / Making Inferences	Recognizing Common and Proper Nouns	Descriptive Poetry	www.s9.com/biography	Biographical Dictionary
	The Moon Bridge	Historical Fiction	Understanding Character / Recognizing Setting	Understanding Punctuation	Expository Persuasive	americanhistory.si.edu/perfectunion	"A More Perfect Union: Japanese Americans and the U.S. Constitution" from Smithsonian
	Our World of Mysteries: Fascinating Facts About the Planet Earth	Science Nonfiction	Making Predictions / Recognizing Cause/Effect	Understanding Compound Words	Expository Descriptive	www.archaeology.org	Archaeology Magazine
	The Phantom Tollbooth	Fantasy	Understanding Plot / Understanding Genre: Fantasy	Using Common Spelling Patterns	Descriptive Narrative	www.scholastic.com	Scholastic
	Sea Otter Rescue: The Aftermath of an Oil Spill	Science Nonfiction	Evaluating Author's Purpose / Understanding Sequence	Reading Unfamiliar Words	Expository Persuasive	www.wcs.org	Wildlife Conservation Society
	Through My Eyes	Autobiography	Recognizing Cause/Effect / Understanding Genre: Autobiography	Recognizing Variations of Words	Poetry Expository	www.civilrights.org	The Leadership Conference on Civil Rights
	You Want Women to Vote, Lizzie Stanton?	Biography	Summarizing / Recognizing Main Idea/Details	Recognizing Antonyms	Persuasive Descriptive	www.nwhp.org	National Women's History Project
X	Anne Frank: Beyond the Diary	Biography	Summarizing / Using Maps	Recognizing Synonyms	Narrative Descriptive	www.ushmm.org	U.S. Holocaust Memorial Museum
	At Her Majesty's Request: An African Princess in Victorian England	Biography	Identifying Facts/Opinions / Drawing Conclusions	Understanding Homophones	Narrative Expository	www.pbs.org/empires/victoria	"Queen Victoria's Empire" from PBS
	Bully for You, Teddy Roosevelt!	Biography	Sequencing / Recognizing Cause/Effect	Understanding Compound Words	Expository Persuasive	www.theodoreroosevelt.org	Theodore Roosevelt Association

Level	Title	Genre	Comprehension Strategies	Phonics and Word-Solving Strategies	Writing Options	Technology	Web Site Sponsor
X	Call It Courage	Fiction	Understanding Character / Relating to Personal Experiences	Reading Words With Suffixes	Graphic Aid / Narrative	pvs.hawaii.org	Polynesian Voyaging Society
	Children of the Wild West	Social Studies Nonfiction	Summarizing / Identifying Problems/Solutions	Using Context	Narrative / Graphic Aid	americanhistory.si.edu	National Museum of American History
	M.C. Higgins, the Great	Realistic Fiction	Making Inferences / Understanding Theme	Recognizing Dialect	Expository / Expository	www.osmre.gov	U.S. Office of Surface Mining
	One More River to Cross: The Stories of Twelve Black Americans	Biography	Comparing/Contrasting / Understanding Genre: Biography	Understanding Variations of Words	Graphic Aid / Persuasive	www.s9.com/biography	Biographical Dictionary
	Out of the Dust	Historical Fiction	Recognizing Setting / Understanding Point of View	Understanding Compound Words	Poetry / Narrative	www.scholastic.com	Scholastic
	Sarah Bishop	Historical Fiction	Understanding Character / Understanding Plot	Reading Unfamiliar Words	Narrative / Persuasive	www.historyplace.com	The History Place
	Summer of Fire: Yellowstone 1988	Nonfiction	Categorizing Information / Recognizing Cause/Effect	Using Common Spelling Patterns	Expository / Persuasive	www.nps.gov	National Park Service
Y	Blizzard!	Social Studies Nonfiction	Paraphrasing / Understanding Historical Context	Understanding Strong Verbs	Expository / Graphic Aid	www.noaa.gov	National Oceanic and Atmospheric Administration
	Castle	Social Studies Nonfiction	Identifying Problems/Solutions / Understanding Sequence	Using Context	Expository / Expository	www.castles.org	Castles of the World
	The Colorado River	Social Studies Nonfiction	Recognizing Setting / Understanding Genre: Nonfiction	Understanding Compound Words	Persuasive / Graphic Aid	www.usgs.gov	U.S. Geological Survey
	The Day Martin Luther King, Jr., Was Shot: A Photo History of the Civil Rights Movement	Social Studies Nonfiction	Drawing Conclusions / Understanding Concepts	Understanding Punctuation	Graphic Aid / Expository	www.civilrights.org	The Leadership Conference on Civil Rights
	I Am an American: A True Story of Japanese Internment	Biography	Identifying Cause/Effect / Relating to Personal Experiences	Reading Words With Prefixes and Suffixes	Graphic Aid / Narrative	americanhistory.si.edu/perfectunion	"A More Perfect Union: Japanese Americans and the U.S. Constitution" from Smithsonian
	My Brother Sam Is Dead	Historical Fiction	Understanding Character / Understanding Point of View	Distinguishing Between Direct and Indirect Quotations	Narrative / Expository	americanhistory.si.edu	National Museum of American History
	Restless Spirit: The Life and Work of Dorothea Lange	Biography	Understanding Genre: Biography / Understanding Character	Working With Vowel Patterns	Narrative / Descriptive	www.photographymuseum.com	The American Museum of Photography
	Seeing Earth From Space	Science Nonfiction	Recognizing Main Idea/Details / Using Illustrations in Informational Texts	Reading Words With Prefixes	Expository / Persuasive	earth.jsc.nasa.gov	"Earth from Space" from NASA
	Tales Mummies Tell	Social Studies Nonfiction	Identifying Main Idea/Details / Making Predictions	Reading Words With Greek and Latin Roots	Narrative / Graphic Aid	www.virtual-egypt.com	Virtual-Egypt.com
	Tales of Real Escape	Biography	Understanding Genre: News Report / Understanding Story Development	Reading Words With Prefixes	Expository / Descriptive	www.nps.gov/alcatraz	Alcatraz Island
Z	Black Beauty	Fiction	Understanding Point of View / Understanding Sequence	Reading Difficult Words	Narrative / Persuasive	www.aspca.org	American Society for the Prevention of Cruelty to Animals
	City: A Story of Roman Planning and Construction	Social Studies Nonfiction	Understanding Steps in a Process / Using Diagrams	Using Context	Persuasive / Descriptive	www.planning.org	American Planning Association
	The Day the Women Got the Vote: A Photo History of the Women's Rights Movement	Social Studies Nonfiction	Categorizing Information / Recognizing Cause/Effect	Reading Words With Suffixes	Graphic Aid / Persuasive	www.nwhp.org	National Women's History Project
	Great Escapes of World War II	Social Studies Nonfiction	Comparing/Contrasting / Identifying Facts/Opinions	Recognizing Variations of Words	Expository / Descriptive	www.historyplace.com	The History Place
	The History of Emigration from China & Southeast Asia	Social Studies Nonfiction	Comparing/Contrasting / Using Maps	Reading Words With Prefixes	Expository / Expository	www.camla.org	The Chinese American Museum
	The Adventures of Tom Sawyer	Fiction	Understanding Character / Making Predictions	Using Context	Narrative / Play	www.scholastic.com	Scholastic
	Treasure Island	Fiction	Understanding Plot / Understanding Chapters	Using Context	Expository / Narrative	www.nationalgeographic.com/pirates	"Pirates!" from National Geographic
	Triumph on Everest: A Photobiography of Sir Edmund Hillary	Social Studies Nonfiction	Summarizing / Understanding Main Idea/Details	Reading Words With -ed	Expository / Expository	www.nationalgeographic.com	National Geographic
	We Shall Not Be Moved: The Women's Factory Strike of 1909	Social Studies Nonfiction	Identifying Problems/Solutions / Understanding Main Idea/Details	Reading Words With Suffixes	Persuasive / Narrative	www.dol.gov	U.S. Department of Labor
	Where the River Runs: A Portrait of a Refugee Family	Biography	Recognizing Cause/Effect / Comparing/Contrasting	Reading Figurative Language	Descriptive / Expository	www.pbs.org/kcet/newamericans	The New Americans web exhibition from PBS

Essential Element	Key Ideas—National Reading Panel
Phonemic Awareness Instruction in Guided Reading • Children use their beginning connections between letters and sounds to check on their reading. They notice mismatches. They use letter-sound information to know how words begin. • Teachers prompt children to make their reading "look right."	"Phonemic awareness instruction is not a complete reading program; it cannot guarantee the reading and writing success of your students. Long lasting effects depend on the effectiveness of the whole curriculum." (3, p. 9) "Phonemic awareness instruction does not need to consume long periods of time to be effective. In these analyses, programs lasting less than 20 hours were more effective than longer programs." (2, p. 2–6) "In addition to teaching phonemic awareness skills with letters, it is important for teachers to help children make the connection between the skill taught and their application to reading and writing tasks." (2, p 2–33)
Phonics Instruction in Guided Reading • Teachers select texts that, along with high frequency words that are available to students, offer opportunities to use phonics skills. • As they introduce texts, support reading, and revisit the text after reading, teachers bring children's attention to features of words and strategies for decoding words. • Children apply word solving strategies to reading continuous texts. • Teachers explicitly demonstrate how to take words apart and apply phonics principles to new words children meet in continuous text. • Teachers explicitly teach phonics principles through word work after the text is read. Word work sessions are connected to a phonics continuum. • Teachers prompt children to use phonics skills to take words apart while reading.	"Children need opportunities to use what they have learned in problem solving unfamiliar words that they encounter within continuous text. They use word solving strategies to take words apart while keeping the meaning in mind." (3, p. 18) "Reading words accurately and automatically enables children to focus on the meaning of text." (3) "Programs should acknowledge that systematic phonics instruction is a means to an end. Some phonics programs focus primarily on teaching children a large number of letter-sound relationships. These programs often do not allot enough instructional time to help children learn how to put this knowledge to use in reading actual words, sentences, and texts. Although children need to be taught the major consonant and vowel letter-sound relationships, the also need ample reading and writing activities that allow them to practice this knowledge." (3, p. 17)
Fluency Instruction in Guided Reading • Texts are selected to be within students' control so that they know most of the words and can read fluently (with teaching). • The teacher introduces the text to support comprehension and connections to language. • Teachers draw students' attention to elements of words that will help them recognize or solve them rapidly.	"If text is read in a laborious and inefficient manner, it will be difficult for the child to remember what has been read and to relate the ideas expressed in the text to his or her background knowledge." (1, p. 22) "Repeated and monitored oral reading improves reading fluency and overall reading achievement." (3, p. 11) "It is important to provide students with instruction and practice in fluency as they read connected text." (3, p. 23) "Word recognition is a necessary but not sufficient condition for fluent reading." (3, p. 30) "Fluency is not a stage of development at which readers can read all words quickly and easily. Fluency changes, depending on what readers are reading, their familiarity with the words, and the amount of their practice

<ul><li>Teachers help children to understand and use the language patterns that may be found in written text.</li><li>Children use word recognition and comprehending strategies in an orchestrated way while reading or rereading a text silently or orally.</li><li>Teachers provide explicit demonstrations and instruction in reading fluency.</li><li>Teachers prompt for fluency when children are reading aloud.</li><li>Children engage in repeated oral readings to work for fluency.</li></ul>	with reading text." (3, p. 23) "By listening to good models of fluent reading, students learn how a reader's voice can help written text make sense." (3, p. 26) "Fluency develops as a result of many opportunities to practice reading with a high degree of success. Therefore, your students should practice orally rereading text that is reasonably easy for them—that is, text containing mostly words that they know or can decode easily." (3, p. 27)
Vocabulary Instruction in Guided Reading <ul><li>Texts are selected so that students know most of the words but there are a few new words to provide opportunities for learning.</li><li>The teacher introduces the text to support comprehension, with specific attention to concepts and words.</li><li>Students read the text silently or orally with teacher support.</li><li>After reading, students and teacher discuss the meaning of the text, with further discussion of word meanings if needed.</li><li>The teacher teaches for processing strategies, which may include both word recognition and how to determine word meanings.</li><li>Children may extend the meaning of the text through writing, which often includes attention to vocabulary.</li><li>The teacher provides 1–2 minutes of pre-planned word work which helps students attend to word parts and word meanings (affixes, word structure, homophones, synonyms, etc.)</li></ul>	"Extended instruction that promotes active engagement with vocabulary improves word learning." (3, p. 36) "Teaching specific words before reading helps both vocabulary learning and reading comprehension." (3, p. 36) "Repeated exposure to vocabulary in many contexts aids word learning." (3, 36) "Conversations about books help children to learn new words and concepts and to relate them to their prior knowledge and experience." (3, p. 35) "…the larger the reader's vocabulary (either oral or print), the easier it is to make sense of the text." (1, p. 13) "…children often hear adults repeat words several times. They also may hear adults use new and interesting words. The more oral language experiences children have, the more word meanings they learn." (3, p. 35)
Comprehension Instruction in Guided Reading <ul><li>Teachers select texts that readers can process successfully with supportive teaching.</li><li>The teacher demonstrates effective strategies for comprehending text.</li><li>In the introduction to the text, the teacher explains words and concepts and assures that students activate their own prior knowledge.</li><li>Students have the opportunity to apply a range of strategies in response to the demands of texts.</li></ul>	"Comprehension is defined as 'intentional thinking during which meaning is constructed through interactions between text and reader' (Harris & Hodges, 1995). Thus, readers derive meaning from text when they engage in intentional, problem solving thinking processes. The data suggest that text comprehension is enhanced when readers actively relate the ideas represented in print to their own knowledge and experiences and construct mental representations in memory." (1, p. 14) "In general, the evidence suggests that teaching a combination of reading comprehension techniques is the most effective. When students use them appropriately, they assist in recall, question answering, question generation, and summarization of texts. When used in combination, these techniques can improve results in standardized comprehension tests." (1, p. 15) "Text comprehension can be improved by instruction that helps readers use specific comprehension strategies." (2, p. 49)

• Students expand strategies by applying them, with teacher support, to texts that are more difficult than they could read independently. • Teachers help children extend their understandings through using oral language and writing. • Teachers help children extend their understanding through using graphic organizers to understand underlying text structures. • While teachers are working with children in small groups, other children read independently the books that they have previously read.	"Text comprehension can be improved by instruction that helps readers use specific comprehension strategies." (3, p.9) "Graphic organizers illustrate concepts and interrelationships among concepts in a text, using diagrams or other pictorial devices. Regardless of the label, graphic organizers can help readers focus on concepts and how they are related to other concepts." "Comprehension strategies are not ends in themselves; they are means of helping your students understand what they are reading." (3, p. 6) "Help your students learn to use comprehension strategies in natural learning situations—for example, as they read in the content areas." (3, p. 65) "Readers must know what most of the words mean before they can understand what they are reading." (3, p. 45) "Children learn many new words by reading extensively on their own. The more children read on their own, the more words they encounter and the more word meanings they learn." (3, p. 35) "Teachers not only must have a firm grasp of the content presented in text, but also must have substantial knowledge of the strategies themselves, of which strategies are most effective for different students and types of content and of how best to teach and model strategy use." (1, p. 16)
Motivation Support in Guided Reading • Teachers select books that will be interesting to children. • Teachers introduce texts in a way that engages interest and motivation.	"Few if any studies have investigated the contribution of motivation to the effectiveness of phonics programs, not only the learner's motivation to learn but also the teacher's motivation to teach. The lack of attention to motivational factors by researchers in the design of phonics programs is potentially very serious…Future research should…be designed to determine which approaches teachers prefer to use and are most likely to use effectively in their classroom instruction." (2)

The ideas in this chart are referenced to the following documents:

(1) National Institute of Child Health and Human Development. 2001. *Report of the National Reading Panel: Teaching Children to Read: An Evidence-Based Assessment of the Scientific Research Literature on Reading and Its Implications for Reading Instruction.* Washington, DC: National Institutes of Health.

(2) National Institute of Child Health and Human Development. 2001. *Report of the National Reading Panel: Teaching Children to Read: An Evidence-Based Assessment of the Scientific Research Literature on Reading and Its Implications for Reading Instruction: Report of the Subgroups.* Washington, DC: National Institutes of Health.

(3) Armbruster, B.B., Lehr, F., & Osborn, J. 2001. *Put Reading First: The Research Building Blocks for Teaching Children to Read, Kindergarten through Grade 3.* Washington, DC: U.S. Department of Education.

[i] "Readers must know what most of the words mean before they can understand what they are reading." (*Put Reading First*, p. 45)

[ii] "Beginning readers use their oral vacabulary to make sense of the words they see in print…Readers must know what most of the words mean before they can understand what they are reading." (*Put Reading First*, p. 45)

BIBLIOGRAPHY

Fountas, Irene, and Pinnell, G.S. (1996). *Guided Reading: Good First Teaching for All Children*. Portsmouth, NH: Heinemann.

Fountas, Irene, and Pinnell, G.S. (2001). *Guiding Readers and Writers, Grades 3–6*. Portsmouth, NH: Heinemann.

Fountas, Irene, and Pinnell, G.S., eds. (1999). *Voices on Word Matters*. Portsmouth, NH: Heinemann.

Pinnell, Gay Su and Fountas, I.C. (1999). *Matching Books to Readers: A Leveled Book List for Guided Reading, K–3*. Portsmouth, NH: Heinemann.

Pinnell, Gay Su and Fountas, I.C. (1998). *Word Matters: Teaching Phonics and Spelling in the Reading/Writing Classroom*. Portsmouth, NH: Heinemann.

Pinnell, G.S., Pikulski, J.J., Wixson, K.K., Campbell, J.R., Gough, R.B., and Beatty, A.S. (1995). *Listening to Children Read Aloud: Data from NAEP's Integrated Reading Performance Record (IPRR) at Grade 4*. Report No. 23-FR-04 Prepared by Educational Testing Service under contract with the National Center for Education Statistics, Office of Educational Research and Improvement, U.S. Department of Education. (p. 15)

RESEARCH AND VALIDATION

A strong pattern of rising scores has been found in schools where daily guided reading has been combined with phonics and word study minilessons and daily writing workshop. For further information, see:

Williams, Jane. 2002. The power of data utilization in bringing about systemic school change. *Mid-Western Educational Researcher*, 15, 4–10.

Williams, E.J., Scharer, P., & Pinnell, G.S. 2000. *Literacy Collaborative 2002 Research Report*. Columbus, OH: The Ohio State University.

Scharer, P., Williams, E.J., & Pinnell, G.S. 2001. *Literacy Collaborative 2001 Research Report*. Columbus, OH: The Ohio State University.